PLAYING WITH
FIRE

PLAYING

WITH

FIRE

THE ART OF CHOPPING
AND BURNING WOOD

PAUL HEINEY

The History Press

First published 2017

The History Press
The Mill, Brimscombe Port
Stroud, Gloucestershire, GL5 2QG
www.thehistorypress.co.uk

© Paul Heiney, 2017

The right of Paul Heiney to be identified as the Author
of this work has been asserted in accordance with the
Copyright, Designs and Patents Act 1988.

British Library Cataloguing in Publication Data.
A catalogue record for this book is available from the British
Library.

ISBN 978 0 7509 7994 8

Typesetting and origination by The History Press
Printed in Turkey

Contents

The glory of
the roaring
wood fire.

Introduction

AUTUMN, WITH ITS promise of wood fires to come, is the finest season of the year for me. It is when I try to take an informed glance at the woodpile and reckon if it is up to the job of seeing me through the winter. Is there kindling in the box, and is it dry? I will take random logs and sniff them, and feel their weight in my hand, guessing how much flame-retarding moisture is still hidden within. It is the first of the winter games I play with nature. If she wins I stay cold, if I win then I have all the comforts a wood fire can give.

Then, like a child longing for Christmas, I start looking at the calendar and see the winter months getting closer. I begin to wonder when the temperature will drop to that magic, undefined figure when I can declare it time to light the first fire of the season. Like the artist who has arranged his colours on his palette, I have prepared my wood as best as I know how and I am once again ready for the artful business of playing with fire.

All summer I will have missed the effort that wood burning demands: the fetching of logs, the striking of the match, the careful building of the logs on the grate, the saying of a silent prayer until the kindling has taken hold and the first log begins to smoulder. I hate it when the place has been devoid of the smell of wood and woodsmoke all summer. It is as if an old friend has been banished from the household. Once the first fire is lit, I will go outside to taste the first whiff of woodsmoke that creeps gently at first from the chimney, and then gathers momentum before disappearing completely as the fire gains heat. That is how I like to reconnect

Every creature in the house loves the warmth of burning wood.

and, while I know that sniffing this grey fog for too long is probably bad for my health, that small downside is nothing compared to the soaring of my mood. The church should be jealous of the spiritual uplift a bit of burning applewood, or pine, can provide.

If this speaks nothing to you, then I doubt you are going to find much here. But let me try and persuade you. Those of us who consider ourselves wood-burners, and those who aspire to be, know that burning wood is one of the most fundamental joys of life, as sustaining as the very breath we take. How lucky I am to be able to choose not to heat myself by stabbing my finger at a dreary thermostat, and how sorry I feel for those whose circumstances mean they can never gaze thoughtfully into the embers of a dying fire nor know the warm uplift that only a dancing flame can give.

I have had a hard education in the ways of burning wood. When I first moved out of town to the country and took command of my first wood-burning stove, I might as well have been presented with a vintage steam engine for all I understood of its flues, dampers and doors. I guessed there was some science to this, but in those pre-internet days information was not so readily to hand, and so much of my learning was done on the job.

In the matter of wood I was even more ignorant. In fact, I can remember buying one of my early loads of logs from a cheeky lad who dropped them on the drive and then quickly disappeared, suspiciously. Had I known anything about firewood at all, alarm bells would have rung when I saw that green leaves were still sprouting from it and that, far from it being seasoned, sap still flowed from it like water from a running tap. It is difficult to learn the subtle ways of a stove when the only thing your smouldering wood will give you is a depressing sizzle, while you are craving heat. There is no snub greater than that given by a heartless fire; it is telling you that you have no idea what you are doing, you should go away and get some understanding of burning wood, and only then come back and bother me with your match when you have learned a thing or two.

Having been brought up in a home not far from the coal mining areas of South Yorkshire, from an early age I was no stranger to the joys of the dancing flame. There was hardly a day when there wasn't an open fire blazing in our house, usually with coal nicked from the power station where my father worked. I learned that flame was not only warm it was soothing too, and it made a child feel good, and the dog and cat calm.

My grandmother was a demon for an open fire and had a pensioner's flat which housed a coal fireplace with a built-in oven beside it – a kind of kitchen range with a large warming area above. It was without doubt the largest item in the flat and commanded everyone's attention and respect, which was willingly given for like all fires it was the heart of the home. These ranges were common in the 1950s. A lot of council houses had them, and they required frequent applications of Zeebrite to keep them shining black. My granny could play this fireplace like a musical instrument, making a song and a dance of it by pulling mysterious levers to direct the

The ever welcoming, ever soothing log fire.

flames from the chimney to the underside of the oven, bending the heat and flame to her will. Never was a bit of heat wasted. When the fire was red hot she would rake the embers and present roasted shoulder of pork to it, creating the crispest bubbling crackling. Then, not wanting to waste so much as a therm of heat, a bowl of bread dough would hit the warming shelf till it fluffed and rose, by which time a shift of the dampers had the oven hot enough to bake it into fresh rolls. It was always lit with newspaper and sticks, and if it was a still day or the draught was somehow poor and the fire wouldn't 'draw' then a shovel would be placed vertically in front of the fire and a newspaper stretched across it, which forced air to enter only through the grate. It always worked, and to my surprise the newspaper never caught fire.

We survived the bitter winter of 1963 in front of that fire, a winter when the sea froze over, and which broke records in terms of cold and longevity. Grandfather, I remember, shuttled between fire and 'coal hole', shovel in hand, dew drop on the end of his nose, hauling jet black coal with the urgency of a man who knew that his flannel shirt was not enough protection from a winter like that.

PLAYING WITH FIRE

I remember there was always a kettle sitting somewhere near the fire, warming itself, singing gently, so as to use less gas when it came time to boil it on the kitchen stove. The shelves in the oven were made of heavy cast iron and on cold nights they would be removed just before bed, wrapped in a blanket and slid into the bed as a warmer. The ranges were eventually replaced with gas fires, known as 'gas misers', and never was there a more apt description. There was never any toast made in front of a fire after that.

My own first wood fire was a different affair; an inglenook in an old Suffolk farmhouse which had not been improved for decades and certainly had no centralised heating system – the nearest thing to a thermostat was opening or closing the kitchen door. Here I learned that romance is one thing and keeping warm is another. There was nothing finer than seeing blazing logs strung across the huge grate, but nothing colder than the cruel, cold draught that comes whistling under the doors, kissing the flames, taking the heat straight up the chimney. I soon learnt that confining your heat in a wood-burning stove was a good idea.

But for all the pleasure I got from burning wood, I was shamefully ignorant of all the things that go to make a roaring fire. I little understood that choice of wood mattered hugely, and that its dryness was a crucial factor. I gave no thought to how chimneys work, and how some would be good while others would always be bad 'uns. I thought stoves were just iron boxes and no more than that. I happily threw logs on the fire, not realising that like any fine structure a fire needed to be carefully and precisely built. Outside, in the garden, fires were more problematic. Bonfires would never go for me, and I invariably ended up with a stinking, smouldering heap which my neighbours – all real countrymen – looked at with pity. When I took to farming and needed to cut hedges, I was completely unaware that if you place the trimmings one way the fire will never burn, but place them properly and they will be consumed until there is hardly a trace of ash remaining. It took an old farmhand who had trimmed farm hedges by hand every year for forty years to teach me that little trick.

But my ignorance went even wider than that. I never gave a thought to the woods or the forest, which is the only source of all the raw materials the fire-maker requires. I knew nothing of how

the forester tended his woods to keep me warm while at the same time keeping his wood alive. In fact, I never gave woods or forest a second thought and certainly didn't appreciate their complexity. Like many innocents, I thought that people who went into woods and cut down trees were somehow 'bad people', completely failing to realise that they were performing the greatest act of kindness for their trees, giving them new life. The axe, which I did not know how to properly swing, remained an item of mystery, and I assumed that my inability to split a piece of wood was a fault on the axe's part, and not on mine. I would never have given a second thought to the axe handle, and how its subtle shape makes it safer and easier to use. I knew that it was best to keep your logs under cover to keep the rain off – that much is obvious even to the complete novice – but I had no appreciation of the fact that properly stacked in a precise geometrical way can turn indifferent wood into good fuel. Did I know there was a way to place logs on a fire that ensures they catch light, and ways of doing it that almost guarantee they never will? I certainly did not.

Many years passed before any of these things crossed my mind. And that is the reason I have written this book. It is not written for you, it is written for me. I have sought out the people who know and understand how fires are made: the forester who grows the wood, the engineers who build our stoves, the blacksmith who hammers out the axe head, and many more. I have been to see them all so they can tell their stories in their own words.

It is my ambition to try and fill a huge gap in my understanding of something so precious but largely unconsidered. For a log fire stands for much more than a few hunks of wood and a waft of flames. It brings together a wider range of skills than could be imagined, and involves a myriad of chemical and biological processes that together make the mind boggle. The story of burning wood is a rich drama of science, biology, mechanics and survival.

Burning wood is not a push-button business. You can start a fire but you have no idea what kind of blaze you will end up with. It carries with it a burden of uncertainty, which in itself is one of its attractions. All you can hope is that all your efforts, and those of countless others who have brought the flame to your hearth, will result in those magical, fleeting, dancing flames, in front of which you can sit and reflect on the sheer magic that is the burning fire.

Dancing
flames when
hot gas meets
cooler air.

1 | How Things Burn

London in 1848. The street lighting, if there is any, is by gas. The incandescent light bulb driven by electricity is being developed in Britain by Joseph Swann, and in America by Thomas Edison, but inside the Royal Institution, where the greatest scientists come to share their discoveries with a wider audience, the rooms are lit either by candles grouped together in chandeliers, or by oil lamps. Into the famous lecture theatre – still widely seen in the modern televised Christmas lectures – steps the great Michael Faraday.

He had, by this time, embraced the recently discovered principles of electromagnetism and constructed the first ever transformer, thereby laying the foundations of many fundamental understandings which remain the cornerstone of physics to this day.

This was an era of rapid scientific and technological advance. Photographs were first produced in 1834, and the typewriter invented in the same year. The pneumatic tyre, anaesthetic, the sewing machine and the science of thermodynamics soon followed. Every passing year brought an advance, many of which survive to this day.

Yet Michael Faraday, one of the most highly regarded scientists of that inventive era, chose not to address the latest advances. Instead, he started his lecture enigmatically:

I have taken this subject on a former occasion, and, were it left to my own will, I should prefer to repeat it almost every year, so abundant is the interest that attaches itself to the subject, so

The white heat of the exploding match.

The ancient candle meets the 'modern' match.

wonderful are the varieties of outlet which it offers into the various departments of philosophy. There is not a law under which any part of this universe is governed which does not come into play and is touched upon in these phenomena.

His subject was 'The Chemical History of a Candle'. It was such an innocent title, but with such profound implications, if Faraday is to be believed. But is he overstating his case? Can there really be sufficient evidence in the gentle, wallowing flame of a candle to suppose that all parts of the universe are governed by the same laws, or at least the laws as they were understood at the time? It is not for me to disagree with Faraday, but for others more qualified to make a judgement.

However, I know that to understand the workings of a flame, and how it produces heat, and where the smoke comes from, and why it shimmers, adds greatly to the already deep pleasures of burning wood. Not only that, but a scientific understanding of combustion explains why wet wood won't burn, and why kindling has to be chopped into small pieces, and why the old saying 'there's no smoke without fire' might not be true in all circumstances – for the perfect fire, as we shall discover, would give off no smoke at all. Understand the flame, and therein lies everything you need to know about lighting a fire.

Take a lingering look at your fire and reflect that the chemical process that is taking place on your hearth is nothing less than the unlocking of the energy the sun bestowed upon the timber as it grew. In fact, it is possible that the energy in your fire was captured by the tree in the years when Faraday was giving his lecture. That is a powerful thought. It is a reminder that the moment of combustion is just the grand finale of one of the most remarkable biological processes on our planet, and it is not for us to screw it up. So let us follow in the great scientist's footsteps and examine the purity of the single candle flame and thereby understand better how our fires work.

But first, the match. Unless we are resorting to bushcraft techniques (see later) most of us will start our fires with a match. This, in itself, is yet another example of pure burning, of using a small amount of energy to release a much larger burst of it. It is such a tiny thing, the flame of a match, and hundreds of matches can be packed into each and every pocket of our clothes, yet a single match can bring down an entire cathedral roof.

The modern match is a comparative newcomer to the business of making fire, having been invented as recently as 1805 by Jean Chancel, a Parisian. The Chinese were employing sticks of wood impregnated with sulphur as far back as the fourteenth century to light lamps, but their development never progressed and each sulphur stick needed an existing flame to light it.

In 1680, the physicist Robert Boyle put his mind to refining the match using the sulphur technique of the Chinese. His idea was to bring about ignition by drawing his match across paper, but it didn't work and he gave up. Instead, he diverted his attention to defining the fundamental relationship between the pressure and volume of gasses, which famously became known as Boyle's Law, and which remains a fundamental principle in the understanding of physics. His time was probably better spent.

Chancel's sticks, it has to be said, seem to have offered very little improvement on the Chinese ones, and his matches were hardly as handy as the small packet you can carry in your pocket. His method

The miraculous chemical processes that are burning wood.

was to coat a stick with potassium chlorate, sulphur and sugar. In an asbestos bottle was held some sulphuric acid, and when the stick was dipped in the acid an almighty exothermic chemical reaction took place generating great heat setting the stick on fire. It was as dangerous, toxic and inconvenient a way of producing a flame as could be imagined. Needless to say, it didn't catch on.

The first friction match was the work of an English chemist, John Walker of County Durham, whose breakthrough moment was the realisation that the necessary chemical reaction to initiate combustion could be ignited by a spark, and that spark could be simply created by friction between the match and an abrasive surface. Walker's matches contained potassium chlorate, antimony trisulphide and sugar, all held together in gum. They were lit by rubbing them across sandpaper. The main problem with his match was that the fire tended to detach itself from the head of the match, and after several carpets were destroyed many domestic fires were blamed on this new invention and matches were consequently banned in France and Germany.

There were many subsequent experiments leading to significant developments, the most important being the discovery that the use of white phosphorus made for a much safer match – phosphorous needs little energy to light it – but concerns about its effect on public health eventually led to white phosphorous being banned. It was a Swede, Johan Lundström who showed that by using red phosphorous all objections were overcome, and by 1858 he was producing 12 million boxes of matches a year. The match has never looked back.

The modern match has a rich cocktail of ingredients, all of which are necessary because phosphorous alone will not produce a flame for long enough to be useful. A modern match works like this: the initial burst of energy from the combustion of the phosphorous breaks down potassium chlorate which releases oxygen, necessary if the flame is to flourish. This oxygen gives support to the igniting sulphur, which keeps the flame going, otherwise it would quickly go out. The head of the match also contains powdered glass to ensure sufficient spark-producing friction when the match is struck, this energy being used to convert the red phosphorous into white phosphorus, which is highly volatile and reacts with the oxygen in turn, leading to ignition. To keep the match burning, the stick can also be impregnated with candle wax.

There is pleasure to be had in just watching the striking of a match, seeing it burst into life, its transition into flame followed not long after by its death. The Danish storyteller Hans Christian Anderson wrote the story of a girl's hopes and dreams after she lit match after match to warm her as she tried in vain to sell her matches on the cold winter streets of Denmark. It was called 'The Little Match Girl'. Once the last match has been lit, and its flame dies, so she dies too. This was one writer's take on the poignancy and inspiration to be found in the writhing of a dying flame. Candle flames were a preoccupation of Anderson from an early age. One of his earliest works, written when he was a schoolboy and only recently discovered, was a short 700-word story called 'The Tallow Candle', about a candle which suffered from lack of self-esteem. The candle was ignored and neglected before its natural beauty was recognised, enhanced once it was lit. Michael Faraday must surely have been bewitched by flame too, or why would he elevate the burning of the candle to philosophical status?

Mystical elements of flame apart, the science itself is worth understanding so that each time you light your fire you can remind yourself of the magic you are performing. Fire works as follows: without three fundamental ingredients, fuel, heat and oxygen, you will never make fire. In the case of the candle, the fuel is wax. The heat that starts the chemical reaction is the flame of the match with which you light it. Oxygen we take for granted but in the case of wood a plentiful supply of oxygen, which might be provided by a draught, is required. You could not light a candle in the vacuum of space, nor could you create a conventional-looking flame because it is gravity that causes hotter air to rise and cooler to fall, and in a zero gravity environment neither of these things will occur. The result is that all the products of combustion would hang around the flame, smothering it, and it would go out.

Back on earth, on applying a match to the wick of the candle, a small quantity of the wax melts. By capillary action the molten wax climbs up the wick. Because the quantity of wax in the wick is small, it does not require much heat to start breaking the wax, which is a hydrocarbon, into hydrogen and carbon. If there were no wick, the quantity of heat required to produce the same effect in a lump of wax would be greater than a single match could provide, so the wick teaches us that small burns more easily than large, which is why we shall eventually cut our fire-starting kindling into slithers and not chunks.

The vaporised hydrocarbon wax has now become hydrogen and carbon and both are drawn upwards, because hot air rises. They then combine with the oxygen in the air, which in turn produces four by-products: water vapour, carbon dioxide and, most usefully, heat and light.

'LOOK AT HOW A SINGLE CANDLE CAN BOTH DEFY AND DEFINE THE DARKNESS.'

ANNE FRANK

But why does the candle keep burning when you take the match away? Simply because that initial burst of heat is enough to melt a little more wax, which again rises the length of the wick, going through a vaporisation process, producing more heat, melting more wax, and so on. Without a wick a candle would not work.

It doesn't always go smoothly. A candle flame can hesitate, and if it is insufficiently hot to melt the wax then the flame will go out. Or too much wax might be produced, or there may be insufficient air. What happens then is that the flame starts to smoke, or gives off unburnt carbon particles, producing soot. This is because the combustion has not been complete.

Once your candle is burning with a steady flame, look at it more closely. There are three distinct bands of colour. At the top is the large, yellow portion, which we tend to think of as the flame. Below that is a brown, or orange, section and this sits on an area at the bottom of the flame, which is bright blue. It is in this bright blue section that the hydrocarbons (molten wax) start to break down into hydrogen and carbon, and because there is plenty of oxygen here the hydrogen reacts with the oxygen to produce water vapour. A little of the hot carbon will also react with the oxygen to produce carbon dioxide, but the carbon has more important business to conduct as it moves up the flame. In the brown zone, where the temperature can reach 1,000°C, the carbon particles start to burn and they continue to get hotter as they enter the yellow zone where, at 1,200°C, they start to ignite and give off light, producing the observable flame.

Firewood follows the candle's example and needs heat to start the reaction. Instead of wax providing the hydrocarbons, in the case of wood it is cellulose that is contained within its structure. Cellulose is the most abundant organic compound in the world and makes

up 50 per cent of every piece of wood. It has no taste, is odourless, you find it in paper and cardboard, and it is what cellophane is made from. It is also used as an additive by the food industry as it adds fibre and effectively bulks up the product, making it cheaper to produce, and weight for weight reduces fat. If you buy grated cheese in a bag, the reason the flakes don't stick together is because cellulose has been added. You might think this is cheating; you thought you were buying cheese, not wood.

From the wood-burner's point of view, the crucial fact is that wood has to reach 150°C before organic cellulose can break down. But before you can do anything you must get rid of the water content; we all know the effect that water has on fire. This will not occur until the wood reaches 100°C, the boiling point of water, when it starts to evaporate. Once that process has started, the next stage is to get the cellulose to decompose.

There are three products of wood combustion. Under the effect of heat, wood gives off volatile gases consisting of hydrogen, carbon and oxygen. Taken together we call them smoke. The carbon element, apart from the small amount of it in the smoke, is known as char – it gives its name to charcoal and the word 'charred'. It's the black, dirty bit left in the grate. Charcoal is, incidentally, wood from which all the volatile elements have been removed, which is why charcoal burns with no flame. That leaves the ash, which is all the other grey, dusty bits, calcium carbonate forming a large proportion but also potash and trace elements such as iron, zinc and copper. This is why wood is often added to compost heaps to provide added nutrients.

The next stage in the wood-burning process is for the volatile gases to start to break apart and this happens around 260°C. Once the molecules have broken apart, the atoms of hydrogen and carbon recombine with the oxygen to produce water and carbon dioxide and this is the process we called burning. Most importantly, it is this reaction which gives off heat, which, in turn, keeps the fire going, in exactly the same way that the molten wax keeps the candle flame alive. As the carbon atoms get hotter they, and other atoms, start to emit light, and this is the flame that you see.

A flame varies in its colours, of course, being bright yellow in some parts and a dull orange in others. This is a representation of the varying temperatures within the flame itself.

To keep a fire blazing the reaction has to kept going, and so once the initial piece of wood is burning others have to be brought up to temperature in turn. This is why a fire made with one piece of wood will never burn, for no single match can provide enough energy to create the combustive reaction in a single chunk of wood. It also explains why we use small pieces of wood to start a fire for we are multiplying the energy as we go. It works like this: a little energy from a match can provide enough energy to get the kindling going, then with that initial energy from the kindling we can ignite the first piece of wood, which in turn passes on sufficient energy to ignite the next. The crucial point in making a fire is the temperature at which the cellulose starts to break down into the highly flammable carbon and hydrogen. Until you get to that point, you will not have a fire. It is obvious that the larger the piece of wood, the more energy is required to get it to that point. You could start a fire with a whole tree trunk, but imagine the number of

matches it would require. How much more quickly you can make fire with a thin sliver of dry wood and only a small flame to start the process.

It is worth watching intently the beginnings of a fire, for all this science is laid out before you within a few minutes. First, set light to a piece of paper, a rich source of cellulose. On first application of a match, the edge of the paper will start to smoulder; there will be no flame but there will be lots of smoke – the product of incomplete combustion. Then, suddenly a flame will appear, seemingly out of nowhere. You have now reached that crucial combustion temperature and proper and efficient burning is taking place. That process complete, you are soon left with a few lumps of almost weightless black carbon.

Some like to talk of the 'fire triangle', which is merely a way of reminding yourself of the three vital ingredients to produce fire: oxygen, heat and fuel. Get them together in the right proportions in the right place and you are playing with fire.

WHY DO FLAMES FLICKER?

A flame would be a dull, diminished thing if it did not flicker, no more than a feeble yellow light. The motion of the flame gives it life, which offers something for our minds to play with. Sometimes flames suggest anger, especially the aggressive flames of a recently lit fire accompanied by spitting and urgent crackle. But a simmering fire which has given up most of its energy and is now on the long, downward slope to its death carries a less athletic but more balletic flame, which dances gently across the hearth, to and fro, as if trying to rock us to sleep.

The flickering of the flame is entirely down to the amount of air that passes over and around it. It is not a constant stream but can come in short-lived waves, or in gusts along with bursts of volatile gases from the decomposing wood. When the flame receives an extra and unexpected 'dose' of oxygen, the carbon particles given off in the combustion process will suddenly burn and a yellow flame will appear. In other parts of the fire, where oxygen is in short supply, the flames will die. To prove this, all you have do is blow on a fire and watch the flames come to life; stop your blowing and the flames will die.

2 | The First Flames

IT IS MAN'S ability to make fire that sets him apart from all other creatures on our planet, although early man might not have seen it that way. Long before it became a friend that warmed and fed us, fire was feared as an enemy or worshipped as a God. Only later did it become part of our domestication.

Where did fire come from? The ancient Greeks said that Prometheus, the creator of mankind, stole it from the gods on Mount Olympus; Native Americans said it was stolen from evil spirits by a wolf or a woodpecker; Pacific islanders say it came from heaven in the beak of a bird.

When did humans first start to control fire, and harness its properties in order to stay alive? Charred wood and bones dating from the Stone Age, 500,000 years ago, have been found in caves in China and these form the earliest evidence of man's controlled use of fire and flame, although it will have been observed in the eruption of volcanoes and the burning of vegetation as the hot lava flowed.

There's no denying the importance of harnessing this fundamental life force, nor its profound consequences by providing heat and the ability to cook food; the domestication of fire is truly one of the greatest junctions along the road of human development, as fire raged through ever facet of developing life. By providing heat through cold nights, fire allowed humans to roam wider across the world to places where they would otherwise have starved; they could now set fire to scrub land, clearing it to make hunting easier.

Eventually, heat gave them the ability to melt and forge metals and create tools. The vital protection that fires gave brought social groups together to gather fuel, and societies were born around an open fire. The link between the social campfires of early man and the family feel of the modern domestic fireplace remains direct and important.

Fire also brought with it social standing, for so important did it become that those who had control over fire ranked higher than all others. Fire-makers were held in the highest esteem, for in their hands was more than the mere ability to create flame; they held the skill that provided the driving force for life itself. If you really want to put a date on it, scholars tell us that about 1.7 million years ago *homo erectus* learned to harness the power of the flame across the globe in Asia, Africa and Europe, and we must accept their scholarly conclusions.

Recent research in Israel has uncovered the use of controlled fire in ancient caves dating back 350,000 years, certainly before the time of 'modern humans'. Researchers from Haifa University found flints that showed exposure to fire and concluded that although early species of man might have used fire for some million years before that, here was evidence, for the first time, that it was being used in a controlled way. That ability to cook food, it is argued, allowed for faster and greater brain growth since cooked food provides 30 per cent more energy than raw food. Cooked food is also softer to eat, which meant that those who had lost their teeth and their ability to chew would still be able to feed themselves and survive. Fire made mankind more intelligent and enabled him to live longer.

Of course, fire itself existed long before humans. In the early development of our planet, when it was no more than a chemistry set, flame, whether created by spontaneous combustion, explosion or lightning, played a vital part in inducing that cocktail of chemicals into producing reactions, thus creating new compounds, amongst them the building blocks of our eventual lives. Man did not invent fire, it was fire that invented man. It was man's great triumph to learn how to control it and develop it for his own evolutionary needs.

'THE SPREAD OF CIVILISATION MAY BE
LIKENED TO A FIRE; FIRST, A FEEBLE
SPARK, NEXT A FLICKERING FLAME, THEN
A MIGHTY BLAZE, EVER INCREASING IN
SPEED AND POWER.'

NIKOLA TESLA, ENGINEER AND PHYSICIST

Now, a million years later, the ownership of fire and flame and the skills need to control it rule the world more than ever before, even if that fire is concealed in the internal combustion engine, the power station or the heating boiler. Fire has changed its visible forms but society still clings to it for survival in exactly the same way as ancient man gathered round his open fire at night to feed and strengthen himself.

If you have the skills to create fire for yourself, you are holding the most magical power in your hands, and with patience and a little understanding you can make a direct connection with mankind of a million years ago. There are few other ways in which something as profound can be achieved.

For an early lesson in fire-making, we can go back just over 5,000 years to the oldest known fire-maker of whom we have direct evidence, and whose fire-making equipment we can observe and copy.

He has been nicknamed Ötzi, because his body was found by two climbers in the Ötzi alpine region on the borders of Italy and Switzerland, in 1991. The discovery, at first thought to be the body of a recently missing climber, on careful examination revealed itself to be the remarkably preserved remains of a 5,000-year-old hunter-gatherer, a man of the mountains. No single find has given us so much information about that period of history. Modern analytical techniques have been harnessed to determine the contents of his stomach (deer meat and bread), the nature of his clothes (a cloak of woven grass, leather loin cloth and shoes), the make up of his blood (same as ours), his meeting with death (possibly murder or religious sacrifice), all preserved in the ice for 5,000 years and only revealed when a portion

of the ice melted away to reveal Ötzi's mummified remains. It is the fact that he died on the mountain and had no formal burial that makes the find remarkable, for it is usual in all cultures to choose a burial spot in soil which will quickly allow the body to decompose. In Ötzi's case, he was preserved exactly as he fell in the snow and ice where desiccation in the cold, dry air created these remarkable remains. Also, had it been a burial, we would not have had an insight into how he was clothed, his tools, or his way of life, for these valuable artefacts might never have been placed in his grave. Remember, Ötzi was roaming the Alps before the Egyptian pyramids or even Stonehenge were constructed – that's how far back he takes us.

The story of his discovery and the way his secrets were untangled makes for compelling reading, but for our purposes we must concern ourselves with the tools he carried, together with a sophisticated kit for making fires. For us, as fire-lighters, this is Ötzi's most important legacy.

ÖTZI'S AXE

He carried an axe, an essential part of a fire-maker's armoury. Although the axe head was made of copper, a coating that had grown over the years made it appear to be made of iron. For a handle, or shaft, a piece of yew had been chosen where a branch of the tree left the main trunk. In Ötzi's time, the idea that the shaft might pass directly through the head had not been devised (it was only in the few hundreds year BC that this became common in Europe, although the Greeks and Romans may have been using this method much earlier) and so an axe shaft would consist of two wooden parts, lashed together at right angles, the shorter length of wood having the head attached to that. Choosing a piece of timber with a natural right angle bend eliminated one join and gave extra strength. Axes from this period have been found before, but usually the shafts were made of ash or oak, and none had been found complete with axe head. It was not crudely made, as you might imagine it. The carving of the handle had been done such that the shorter length, the haft, was oval in shape while the shaft was circular in cross section maintaining the strength of the original wood whilst providing a secure home for the axe head. The head itself was set into the haft so that only the cutting edge was visible; this gave more security to the head. To keep it in place an adhesive was used called birch tar, or pitch, which is made by heating birch bark in an airtight pot where the bark turns to tar and ashes. Birch tar has been described as 'the all-purpose glue of prehistory'. The axe was finished with strips of leather tied tightly round the haft helping further to keep the blade in place. Remarkably, when the axe was found, it was intact apart from one strip of leather, which had started to unwind, making it the only complete prehistoric axe that has ever been found.

THE RETOUCHER

This is the only known example in the world and looks, at first glance, like a fat pencil. It is made from a branch of a lime tree, cut to 20cm length, one end sharpened pencil-like. Where you might expect to find a lead, you instead discover a length of fire-hardened deer antler. Although there is no record of how this was used, it is thought that it was a device to sharpen a flint tool. Presumably sparks were produced and this might have been a further use for it, although scientists now think this unlikely.

THE BIRCH BARK BOXES

Two small boxes about 20cm deep and wide were found, one of them accidentally crushed underfoot as the body was being exhumed. The boxes, which are still made in that northern part of Italy, were made from a piece of birch bark, sewn into a circle using lime tree bast (a fibre that can be found in the bark and made into twine), and with a circular base sewn in a similar way. What makes the boxes fascinating from the fire-starter's point of view is that one of them was found to be blackened on the inside and contained maple leaves and charcoal fragments. The assumption is that in the birch bark box Ötzi was able to take embers from a previous fire, wrap them tightly in leaves, and transport them to his next camp where the embers could be reignited with a breath or two. Embers could last for several hours when transported in such a way.

THE POUCH

If you can imagine a modern-day 'bum bag' then you have a precise image of Ötzi's pouch in which he carried his kit for making fire. It contained a scraper, two flints and an animal bone, but none of these were for fire-making. For that we have to examine a 'black mass' that was found by forensic examination. This turned out to be the remains of a kind of fungus, *Fomes fomentarius*, known as the 'tinder fungus'. This is commonly found in Europe, where it grows on the bark of infected trees and appears in the shape of a horse's hoof. To turn it into tinder, it must first be removed from the tree to reveal an inner spongy, fibrous layer, which is then dried. It can also be ground into a fine powder. Although it can be ignited with a spark, it does not burst into flame and so some fine kindling is required once the tinder fungus is producing enough heat to ignite it.

When the composition of the black mass in the pouch had been established, further microscopic tests revealed tiny crystals adhering to it. These were yellow/golden in colour and analysed to show that they contained sulphur and iron, making the crystals iron pyrites, otherwise known as fool's gold. Together with the fungus, this was all Ötzi needed to light a fire. Pyrite is not stable and when exposed to air will rapidly oxidise, giving off heat as it does so. If a piece of pyrite is struck with a flint, small pieces of pyrite will be removed, these will rapidly oxidise, get hot and produce a spark. Properly directed onto the tinder, the spark can ignite a fire.

Although the scraper, flints and animal bone don't appear to be directly involved in fire-making, they might have been the tools used to prepare the tinder fungus, which had to be ground until it took on the appearance of cotton wool, providing a greater surface area for the fire to take hold.

With these few pieces of equipment, light, compact and easily carried, Ötzi had the capability to move his fire from one place to the other, using the embers in his beech bark box, or he could light a fire from scratch using the tinder fungus and a spark from the pyrites. Together with a natural skill he would never be without fire; the iceman would never freeze.

3 | Lighting Fires: The Basics

BEFORE YOU EVEN think about striking a spark, or a match, have the following in mind:

Don't light a fire unless you have permission to do so.

Check the surroundings and imagine what would happen if the fire got out of control. Dry grass or conifers nearby could catch light in windy conditions.

You will need a knife and possibly a saw. Are they sharp? Do you know how to use them? Have you a first-aid kit in case of an accident?

Don't light a fire unless you are certain you can put it out. Have water standing by.

Never leave a fire burning after you have finished with it. Make sure it is completely out, even checking for embers which might have been spat out.

Having obeyed all those rules, now imagine yourself as our Alpine hero, Ötzi, with nothing more in your pouch than he carried. How are you going to keep yourself warm and thereby alive? You have the tools but do you have the tricks of the fire-lighter's trade?

'THE FIRE IS THE MAIN COMFORT OF THE
CAMP, WHETHER IN SUMMER OR WINTER,
AND IS ABOUT AS AMPLE AT ONE SEASON
AS AT ANOTHER. IT IS AS WELL FOR
CHEERFULNESS AS FOR WARMTH AND
DRYNESS.'

HENRY DAVID THOREAU

It is a maxim of the bushcraft business – in which you are taken into a woody wilderness and taught to fend for yourself – that you should know the Rule of Threes. It states that:

A human being can survive:
Three minutes without air
Three minutes without a regulated body temperature
Three days without water
Three weeks without food.

Of course, you can go for three months or more without the sight of a fire if you are in the right place at right time, but having the ability to warm yourself to the right temperature for your body to function comes high on the survival list, assuming you are not lucky enough to find yourself abandoned in the tropics.

STARTING FIRES IN WOODS: DAVE WATSON

www.woodlandsurvivalcrafts.com

As it takes a skilled player to get tune out of a stringed instrument, so it takes a bit of skill to light a fire with some of the basic devices that Dave employs. I met him in a forest on the Leicestershire/ Derbyshire border in a glade amongst the ash, beech and birch trees. Here, beneath canvas sheets supported on wooden frames, where camp fires smoulder and steam rises gently from soot-blackened, ever-singing kettles, Dave teaches the practices of woodland survival, and uses the atmosphere of the forest and the intensity of personal survival to bring about profound change in the minds of the people who take his courses. It has the ramshackle look of a refugee camp or the home of a forgotten tribe. Dave's customers like it that way.

He lifts the sturdy black kettle from the glowing embers and brews tea in a tin mug. Smoke wafts through the tent in which

Dave Watson
– the kettle is
always on the
log fire.

we are sitting, then upwards through a makeshift chimney and out into the air to swirl among the trees. Across the other side of encampment there's another fire blazing. This is contained in a small wood stove that can be folded away and packed in the back of a car. In front of it, staring into the flames, his hands clasped around his mug, is a lone figure. 'He's had cancer,' explains Dave. 'He asked me if he could just come up here and sit in the wood, in front of a fire, and get things sorted in his head. Of course, I let him.'

Dave left school 'with little on paper'. 'I was trying to get my head around life. I wanted to know if we evolved or if we were created, that sort of thing. I suppose I was searching for truth, but not through religion. That was stage one. I was going to go into farming, but it didn't seem quite right, and I thought, "what else?"

'I came across outdoor centres, read survival books, did climbing, learned archery. A lot of it I had to work out for myself and couldn't make head nor tail of it at first. Take fire, for example. I had to work out how to choose the wood and perfect the technique. If you don't get it right you can soon become demoralised. This is at the very heart of learning.'

PLAYING WITH FIRE

Taking his own life's learning as an example, Dave now brings the message to young people who are in the most urgent need of finding the direction that he eventually discovered.

'If you build a person when they're young, you set 'em up for life. My job is to equip them and inspire them. I don't turn over huge numbers, perhaps 500 a year, and there's a lot of one-to-one. It's a subtle therapy. They're finding a lot of dissatisfaction in life. They've got all these advanced technologies but no satisfaction, so they look for a destructive way out. What I'm offering them is a constructive way forward. I'll start out by showing them how to light a fire, and they'll mess about. Some have never been to the country before. They might be big and brave in the city but they're not out here; they're often scared of the dark. And do you know why they mess around? It's because they're afraid of succeeding. But I teach them how to, and it dawns on them that if they've got the concept of being able to look after themselves, then they have an understanding of a fundamental core value. It's one that is important, especially to males. I make them sleep in the open, or on hammocks between trees, or in shelters they've built themselves. This is the power of survival, and you can never be quite certain what impact it is going to have on a young person. But I've seen some phenomenal results. One lad came back to me and said, 'Since that course, something happened; something that made sense.' And then Dave leans forwards, shifts the logs beneath the simmering kettle, brings it back to the boil as the fire blazes and crackles, and he makes more tea.

Of all the therapeutic tools at his disposal, the most important is probably the campfire. 'That's when something special happens. There's lots of relaxing, you get an openness and a new quality of conversation. We always get the fire going early, get a brew on, make the fire the centre of things, the focus. For a good campfire you need a wood that's going to give you plenty of heat with no smoke and no sparks. So I'd use pine or spruce to start it, then hazel or birch which would give me lots of good, hot embers for cooking.'

Successful fire-making, according to Dave, is not unlike driving a car – the secret is knowing when to change gear. 'People change gear too soon by putting on bigger logs than the fire can take. Equally, if you load a fire with too much small stuff you can choke it. It's knowing when to change, that's the secret.'

DAVE WATSON'S RULES
FOR A GOOD CAMP FIRE

Make it on dry ground, not on peaty soil or anything that might hold moisture. If it's damp, build it on a platform of split wood or bits of plank. The first embers you create must not fall on damp ground.

Once you have your embers (see below) then have ready some finely split hazel or willow. Larch is also fantastic if you cut it thin – it's full of resin.

The most important thing is to get a good heart of embers.

Then you can build your fire, but remember the car analogy – don't change gear till your fire is up to speed.

If you are making a fire to cook on, make it a long one so you have a hot zone for cooking and a cooler one for sitting round.

The biggest mistakes with any fire are pushing it too hard and using green wood.

If you want the perfect fire for sitting by, burn some oak and cherry and it will give you a lovely scent. Add some ash to that and you've got an all-singing, all-dancing fire. Perfect!

TINDER FOR STARTING FIRES

As any survivalist will tell you, and Dave will agree, good, dry tinder is the secret of any form of fire-making and tinder can be made from anything which will easily catch light and can be found naturally. Look for something with an open structure and therefore a large surface area which will combust easily. As a general rule, anything you use as tinder should be long dead and dehydrated. Anything that has been recently alive will be full of moisture which will inhibit flame. Also, the fluffier the better – surface area is good.

Birch bark shavings are the 'peel' of the birch tree and the thinner you can find them the better – they make good kindling. They are easy to remove from the tree and when peeled off can be as thin as paper. If you find a dead tree of any kind, it is worth hunting around beneath the bark to reveal the inner bark which may be dry and

Good tinder made from very dry grass and flammable down from forest plants.

Dry birch bark peels easily and makes first class tinder.

fibrous. It will need to be torn and made into fibres but you will be rewarded with some of the best, long-lasting kindling.

If you are planning ahead, make yourself some 'tinder balls' by taking cotton wool balls and coat them in Vaseline and carry them in a plastic bag or tin. If no cotton wool, try tampons.

A piece of string made of natural fibres such as jute or sisal can be untwisted to reveal the fibres which you can form into a fluffy ball, and these will make excellent tinder.

Char cloth you can prepare in advance by placing a piece of natural cloth, like cotton from a T-shirt or a piece of denim, in a tobacco tin with a tight-fitting lid and then leaving it in a fire where it will turn to pure carbon – there is no oxygen available to allow it to burn. Make a small hole in the tin to allow any smoke to escape or the tin may blow. Char cloth ignites very easily and makes excellent tinder. Old sacking is a good, natural cloth to use.

Pine needles, grass and hay make good tinder, if bone dry. Grass will work providing it is dead and dried, as in hay. Leaves must be crisp and crackle when you break them. If they are in the slightest bit limp they will not light. Used as tinder, leaves are best if crumbled.

Rotting wood, if it is dry, can be used, as the decaying process allow the fibres to open up exposing a larger surface area for the fire to get hold of.

Lint, or 'fluff' collected from the filter in a tumble dryer with added Vaseline is useful.

The fluff that is known as a 'dandelion clock' is easily ignited. Any plant which gives off fluffy growth can be used, and even the dried seed heads of weeds.

Note that your own hair, or animal fur, will not burn.

THE TINDER STICK

This is a somewhat artistic and satisfying form of tinder requiring a sharp knife, dry wood, and a little practice.

This Christmas tree-like creation sits somewhere between tinder and kindling. If you are in a forest then seek out a piece of dry, dead wood for this will be bone-dry right to the core. If doing this

A tinder stick carved from dry softwood.

at home, a bit of dry softwood such as pine that has been lying in the garage for some time will do the job, and resins in the wood will help the flame take hold.

The object is to produce a bunch of 'feathers' and you will need a sharp knife (and protective gloves if your knife skills are in any way suspect). Start to take long, thin shavings, beginning at one end and coming about a foot down the stick. Don't let the shavings detach. Then take another thin slice, again being careful not to cut so far as to detach it from the stick. When you have done this a couple of dozen times you will have created something that looks a bit like a wooden feather. Having greatly increased the surface area of the stick, it will ignite all that more easily. There are variations. You can simply take repeated thin slivers, parallel to each other; or you can give the wood a turn after every stroke creating more of a bush-like appearance to the stick. The finer you can make the slivers, the more effective the tinder.

KINDLING

Once you have your tinder smouldering, the next stage is to use kindling to build the fire to a strength where it can be loaded with the wood you intend to burn. You'll be familiar with the kindling used to light a wood stove, but for an open fire built under what might be called pioneering conditions you need to be a little more careful in your choice. As you will have understood by now, dryness is as essential in the tinder as in the kindling and the eventual fuel. Splinters of wood, or very fine shavings, are the best, and these can be easily made with a little knife work. Small twigs can be used. If choosing wood to make shavings, use resinous softwood if you can, as this will fire more easily. Pine, for example, is good for this.

Remember to tread gently and not to rush. The big mistake is to pile your kindling too quickly onto the smouldering tinder, a certain way of putting out the precious embryonic fire that you have nurtured.

FAGGOTS

Another form of kindling is the traditional 'faggot' – an old Middle English word meaning a bundle of sticks used as fuel. They still have their uses today as instant fire-starters in the wood-fired ovens beloved of the artisan pizza industry. The making of faggots was a traditional part of a woodman's job and they could be in great demand, often sent up to London by the trainload from southern parts of the country. Depending on the thickness of the twigs that are used, the bundles of thinner, shorter twigs might be called pimps, and the thicker longer ones known as faggots. Faggots and pimps use up wood which might otherwise go to waste. The felling of any tree leaves you with a great deal of brash once all the useful wood has been removed, and there are many uses for this apparently waste product. Some wood owners pile it along boundaries to make a fence to deter deer or muntjac from entering.

Faggots remain useful things and are simple to make and highly effective at giving great heat very quickly, which is why they found

Brash would once have been bundled into faggots.

great favour when wood-fired ovens, in bakeries for example, had to be heated very quickly. The faggot ovens were built of brick or stone with chambers on either side and below. Faggots were stuffed into these chambers then set alight. The faggots were allowed to burn to ash, by which time the intense heat that a seasoned faggot can produce had imparted heat into the brick or stone, and there it stayed long enough for the baker to bake his bread. Once lit, a faggot gave out a great deal of heat – but not for long, so their use on open fires was limited. If a dull fire needed a bit of inspiration, a faggot thrown on it would soon spread joy to the room.

The size of a faggot is strictly laid down in the 1552 Assize of Fuel, which defined wood fuel as being 'assized (decided by a court) into shids, billets, faggots, fall wood and cord wood' – the faggot being a bundle of sticks 3ft in length and 24in in diameter. If you had fifty faggots, then you had a 'load'. A faggot for use on a fire rather than in an oven would have been much shorter.

To make a faggot you need only a sharp billhook with which to trim up the branches to remove side wood, and then a hard surface to use as a chopping block to trim the sticks to length. Any short pieces can be bundled in the middle of the larger ones. Once bundled, they must be stored and thoroughly dried.

It is an old tradition that all guests invited to a house-warming party should bring a faggot with them. Should a younger sister marry before the eldest sister, to avert bad luck she must step over a small faggot when first entering the new home.

In the West Country, an 'ashen faggot', big enough to roll, has been burnt at Christmas since Saxon times – the bundle being tied together with bands of green ash. And as each band is burned away there is a toast and another song.

THE VITAL SPARK

It is well known by all those who were brought up as Scouts that fire can be made by rubbing two bits of stick together, or so they say. The image is fine; the practice is often rather different. To be honest I've never quite believed it, but the theory is quite simple: rubbing creates friction, which creates heat, which makes fire.

However, there are many reasons why you could sit there all day with two sticks, rubbing them together till your arms fell off, and you still wouldn't end up with a blaze. The nature and dampness of the wood is a major factor working against you, but also the sheer strength and staying power needed to keep providing the friction. And even then, after expending all that effort, you do not suddenly get a leaping flame, merely a fragile speck of glowing dust which must then ignite some tinder, which in turn must make more kindling catch before you can claim to have anything approaching a fire. A lot has to go right to create a fire this way, and there is much to go wrong.

THE FIRE PLOUGH

To see if you have the stamina for making fire, test yourself by trying the fire plough method, an ancient method of making fire.

Find a piece of very dry hardwood and split it down until you have a baseboard, no thicker than a chopping board; it needs to be a couple of inches thick.

Using a sharp knife, carve out a groove, no more than about ¼in deep and perhaps a bit wider. At one end of the groove, carve a circular cup into which the hot dust will fall. This will at the end of the baseboard furthest away from you.

For the plough, you will need dry softwood in the form of a stick, one end of which you sharpen till it is like the head of a rounded pencil.

Place the baseboard on a hard surface so that it can't move. Put the tip of the plough into the groove, then apply as much pressure as you can and rub the plough swiftly up and down from one end all the way to the other.

This is hard work and it can be some time before you get anything approaching heat. Persistence is the key. However, if nothing is happening after thirty seconds and you see no smoke, then something is not right and you should adjust the way you are rubbing, or perhaps conclude that the wood is too wet.

If you get as far as smoke you are doing well. You will then see a blackening of the wood along the length of the groove. This is very fine dust, a product of the friction, which is starting to burn, and the tip of the plough will have driven this into the cup you have carved. It should be smoking a little. Give it a gentle blow, or just waft it with your hand to create a gentle breeze, and see if it will glow.

When you are certain it will survive, have your bundle of tinder ready and tip the contents of the cup onto it. Then coax it gently with gentle breaths till it catches light and you have flames. You can now start to make a fire.

THE BOW DRILL

The more friction and the faster you can create it, then the sooner you will get flame. This is the ruling principle of all friction fire-making. The plough method is certainly effective, but man's natural instinct to invent and improve took the plough idea and from it developed the bow drill. It is another kind of friction device and one that a demented cello player might recognise. By wrapping the string of a bow round a vertical stick, it is possible to make it spin quickly as the bow was moved to and fro. If the stick is then pressed against another piece of wood and pressure applied, a great deal of friction can be quickly created.

This was a big step forward, and doubtless a worthwhile development of a simpler friction system where a vertical stick rested on a piece of wood and the stick was rotated to and fro between the palms of the hands. The bow drill is ancient and was described in the Vedas, a body of texts that form the oldest of the Hindu scriptures. The method is still used for lighting sacred fires.

Dave Watson makes (and sells) bow drills which use traditional materials and are made to a pattern unchanged for millennia.

There are four parts to a bow drill. The bow is made from hazel to which is attached the string which can be made from woven nettles, the stalks of which have been stripped of their leaves and stinging hairs, the soft, inner core removed and the outer fibres dried. This can be woven into a very durable string. Elm bark also makes a good string. It can be removed from an elm branch in long slivers, then pulled apart into thin strips and twisted between the fingers into a strong string. A good measure for the bow is to make it the length of your arm. If you are going to be cutting standing wood to make your drill, choose dead wood, but not from the ground where it will have taken up moisture.

The baseboard, sometimes called a hearth board, needs to be made of a light, non-resinous wood, such as lime. Sycamore is good too. Into this baseboard you carve a cup-shaped hole into which the drill will sit.

The drill is a straight length of wood the size of a middle finger. If it's too big then too much strength is needed to turn it and the string will wear quickly. It shouldn't be too long or it will

The simple parts of a bow drill.

After half a minute you should start to see smoke.

The glowing embers from the bow drill are used to light the tinder, with the help of a gentle breath.

be difficult to provide enough downward pressure. It needs to be carved into a domed shape at one end (this will be the lower end) and pencil shaped at the upper end. The domed end is quite important as you want to create the maximum amount of friction and so the shape of the head of the drill should match the cup you have carved in the baseboard. Good wood for the drill would be willow or hazel.

The bearing, which is held in one hand and provides downward pressure on the drill, needs to be able to sit comfortably in the palm of your hand. It could be a flint pebble with a depression in it, a piece of hardwood such as holly or hornbeam. A knee bone from a cow is suitably shaped, and so can be a piece of antler. It is important that this operates with the minimum rather than the maximum friction; otherwise a lot of effort will be wasted. For lubrication fresh leaves can be used; ivy is recommended.

I watched Dave assemble his bow drill, and it seemed unlikely that it might ever produce fire. It was a dank day where nature was doing everything it could to hinder any kind of combustion. I watched him choose his dry spot, then kneel, pressing down hard on the drill which he then 'played' with the bow. 'Get yourself comfortable,' he advises, 'and don't fight it. That's a common mistake. Let the whole thing flow.' It still looked unlikely to my eyes. But that is a common problem amongst first time fire-starters – we are not in proper frame of mind. In the booklet that comes with his kits, Dave's first advice is, 'Be optimistic, be patient, persevere. View this process as a journey and not a fight.'

Accepting his own advice, his journey didn't take long. To my amazement the rounded head of the drill blackened. Not long after fine wisps of smoke started to appear. When Dave thought that the amount of smouldering black dust was sufficient, he withdrew the drill and gently blew across the embers to see if there is enough energy in them for the added oxygen to make them glow. There was. He carefully removed them, breathing gently on them to keep them alight, and placed them on the tinder he has prepared – downy tissue taken from bulrushes surrounded by dry grass. More breaths and the sparks started to fly, rising into the air and falling into the fibres while still glowing. When the first smoke started to appear I felt as if I wanted to cheer. When the smoke eventually gave way to flame,

I felt speechless at the small miracle that had been enacted before my eyes. Dave Watson is right – making fire speaks to the soul.

OTHER SPARKS

Anything that produces a spark will give you a chance of starting a fire. If you have a flint, you can try scraping a steel down one face of it allowing any of the resulting sparks to fall into some kindling, which might be fungus as described above. Once the fungus has taken, you can then build your fire by adding progressively larger pieces of kindling, but starting small so as not to smother any young flame. Remember Dave's advice not to change gear too soon. If you can't find fungus, try cotton wool that has been impregnated with Vaseline.

The Swedish fire steel can be a more reliable source of sparks. It was first invented in 1903 and consists of an alloy of metals which, when struck against steel, produce a spark with a temperature of up to 3,000°C. It was further developed by the Swedish Ministry of Defence in the 1950s, and is a reliable way to get a fire going, even functioning when wet. It comes in two parts: the steel itself and the striker, and by striking the two together a spark is produced. If you have no striker, the back edge of a knife will work just as well.

The smallest steels are good for 2,000 strikes; a large steel might do 12,000. Despite the many claims made for this kind of firelighter and similar ones, it nowhere approaches the efficiency of the simple match.

OUTDOOR FIRES

You can take a pile of wood, or any other dry matter, set it alight, and call it an open fire. You might label it a campfire, or a bonfire. It might be for warmth, for cooking, or merely a device for getting rid of flammable rubbish like twigs or leaves. Fires seem to be simple, but their appearance is deceptive.

Even though these are not fires for survival, they should never be approached casually. A fire knows if your heart is in the job. Treat it

To get this bonfire to go, the branches need to be properly aligned.

with indifference and the fire will soon know and the hissing wood and the billowing smoke will mock you.

Even if you are using a reliable match to produce ignition, without some dry tinder you are not going to get very far. You might want to use newspaper (better if soaked in paraffin wax) if you don't want to take the survivalist route and aren't inclined to collect birch bark and all the other naturally occurring tinders described earlier. Whatever you choose, it needs to be scrupulously dry or you will find yourself frustrated from the outset.

I'm assuming you've chosen a safe and dry spot, on dry bare earth with no risk of nearby vegetation catching light, and that your fire is 15m from any structures like tents or trucks. You can then choose one of several ways in which to build your fire. It can help to dig a fire pit if the ground is suitable, and if you are allowed to do it, for this will contain the fire. A pit also provides something of a firewall if the wind gets up and there's a danger of the fire spreading. It also gives the young fire some shelter from gusts.

The wig-wam method of starting an outdoor fire.

When it is time to put the fire out, you can do so using the soil you dug out in the first place. The pit needs to be only a few inches deep. Too deep and you may have a problem getting a sufficient flow of oxygen to the fire.

THE WIGWAM METHOD

This is probably the most obvious method of starting a fire and for that reason the most commonly used.

Start with your tinder and place it on the ground where you would like the centre of your fire to be. If you are on dry earth which is easily disturbed, you can pull a little of the soil together to create a small platform.

Then take your kindling and build it over the tinder forming a wigwam, but leaving an opening facing into any wind to catch a draught. Start with the thinnest kindling nearest to the tinder

The leaning stick way of starting a fire.

and gradually build the structure using larger pieces of wood as the wigwam expands. The shape of the wigwam encourages the flames upwards.

Set light to the tinder.

Eventually the kindling will burn away and the wigwam collapse but by now you should have arranged your outer layer of firewood – don't make these pieces too big.

THE LEANING STICK

This is a variation on the above method and starts with a piece of kindling stuck into the ground at roughly a 45-degree angle, pointing into the wind. The kindling is then placed around the tinder, but resting against the leaning stick to allow air into the fire to aid combustion. In reality, this operates exactly the same as the wigwam method and is merely a different way of guaranteeing air gets to the centre of the fire. It has the disadvantage that you might need a hammer to get the first stick into the ground.

THE LOG CABIN

This is where you build the kindling around the tinder as if you were surrounding it with a small log cabin.

First build a small wigwam fire, smaller than if you were using a wigwam alone, and then place two pieces of kindling parallel to each other on opposite sides of the wigwam. Then place two more pieces on top of and at right angles to the first two pieces and continue building in this way. The lower pieces of tinder can be heavier than the upper ones, which must be the lightest as these will catch fire first. This is generally reckoned to produce the longest lasting fire. As a rule of thumb, but not to be relied upon, a log burns one hour for every inch of its thickness – a 6in log burning for six hours.

THE UPSIDE-DOWN FIRE

This can be very effective, but trickier if the breeze is gusty as the tinder is more exposed. The advantage is that once the fire is going it needs no feeding as the fire burns progressively downwards, meeting larger and larger logs as it does so. This might make it a good kind of fire if you want to keep it going overnight, for example. Since you can start with logs of whatever size you want, this is a good way of making a substantial fire which you intend to keep burning.

As the name suggests, start with the larger logs at the bottom and then follow the same method for building the log cabin fire but making the pieces of wood smaller as the pile grows until the upper layers are mostly kindling. The tinder then goes on the top. The upside-down fire can sometimes be tricky to get going and the secret is to make a large enough wigwam on the top to ensure the wood below catches well. Unless you can be sure that the first layer beneath the wigwam is going to catch, the fire will stop short there and then.

The log cabin style of starting a fire.

The top down method.

THE LONG LOG FIRE

So called because of the length of the logs you use, which can be as long as a metre, this method produces a long-lasting and robust fire needing plenty of space and giving off lots of heat.

You need three decent-sized logs, the first two you place side by side and an inch apart – it is important that air can get to the heart to fire or it will never burn. Fill the gap between the two logs with a mixture of finely cut kindling and some tinder. When you have lit the kindling and it has caught well, spread it along the gap adding more fuel if you need it, then place the third log lengthways on top of the first two logs, covering the flames that will now be coming from the kindling. The third log should be the largest of the three. The upper log will ignite and so will the lower two with the potential of creating a lot of heat.

Because this fire burns very hot, and consumes a lot of wood in doing so, it is best not considered an everyday kind of fire and should only be lit in places where there is no risk of damage to anything around it, including the soil beneath.

THE STAR FIRE

This is the one you see in cowboy movies. It can make for a long-lasting fire, and a good one for hanging a cooking pot over as the heat is concentrated in quite a small area. Start by making a wigwam fire and have four or six pieces of dry wood ready for when the wigwam is really blazing. Then insert the end of the logs, equally spaced around the fire, and let them catch. As they burn away all you need do is gently push them further into the fire.

Steel fire bowls are becoming increasingly common in gardens and on patios and the star fire is a good way of feeding the fire because as the logs burn down they will tend to slide down the sides of the bowl feeding the fire automatically, if you're lucky.

ONLY GOT ONE LOG?

All these fires need a collection of logs to fuel and feed them, but if you only have one log to hand there is no reason you shouldn't have a hot and long-lasting fire. One-log fires are either Scandinavian or Canadian in origin, suggesting they are based on years of experience gathered by woodsmen working in the cold, high latitudes in freezing winters where a reliable source of heat, even with limited facilities, always needs to be available.

The Canadian Candle, also known as the Swedish Fire Torch, is a one-log fire. To make it you need no more than a single log, some wood shavings or other kindling, and an axe. The joy of the Candle is that you end up with a fire with a flat top, making it ideal for holding a kettle or a frying pan.

Your log might need to be a foot wide and have flat ends so that it will stand upright. You need to make three cuts across the head of it, effectively cutting the log into four or six equal pieces, like the slice of a pie. But – and this is the tricky bit – when you chop the wood don't allow the axe to go all the way through. If your axe skills are uncertain, you can make the cuts with a chainsaw. The log needs to remain intact at the base. If you accidentally split the wood all is not lost. Dig a small hole and set the log into it, effectively holding it together. Into the splits you can now stuff some tinder, plenty of it, which might be paper, wood shavings or birch bark, and some oil if you have some, perhaps from your chainsaw (not petrol). Domestic firelighters will also work. Ignite the kindling. With plenty of room for air to reach the centre of the flames, you will soon end up with a simple, roaring fire on top of which you can place a cooking pot. There is no better example of the difference it makes to a fire to have an efficient chimney combined with a guaranteed draught, which is what you have effectively created. You might get two or three hours of heat from a fire like this.

THE RAAPPANAN TULI FIRE

This is very similar to the Canadian Candle but with subtle variations.

You need a log no longer than 1ft and about 8in in diameter. Split your log in half, then, using an axe, split from the inside thin slivers of wood which you will use as kindling. Make sure this heartwood feels dry or its use as kindling will be limited. You need to choose a broad log to start with because each half in going to have to stand up on its own. As you remove wood for your kindling you will be narrowing the base.

With your axe or knife, start to make cuts on the faces of each half, this being to provide some thin surface area on which the flame can get a hold. Do this the full length of the log till it looks feathered – although not cutting as deep or as long, this is the same process as making the feather stick.

There is an alternative way of doing this and that is the split the log into three parts taking a thinner slice in the middle and feathering both sides of this. The end result will be the same.

Stand up the logs side by side with the gap between them pointing into the wind, supporting them if necessary, and with the feathers pointing downwards. Light the kindling and feed it as it burns away until the two half logs are well and truly alight.

This fire takes its names from Aaro Raappanan, a Finnish rural police chief described as 'a very keen wanderer'.

THE ROCKET STOVE

Again, this is a one-log fire, and very effective, but it needs a few more tools than a woodsman's axe and knife. It starts with a single log about 6in in diameter and a foot long. You will need a drill bit which will cut a 1in hole, and given its size and the length to which you have to go into the log you'll probably need an electric drill on the end of it.

Stand the log on its end and start drilling into the wood until you are about half way down. Make careful note of how far you have drilled because you are now going to turn the log on its side and drill a hole at right angles to the first so that they meet in the centre of the wood. This can be tricky but it is essential that the meeting place of the two holes allow for the free movement of air.

Stand the log upright. You will now need a piece of very dry kindling, not much fatter than a drinking straw, helped along with a bit of paraffin wax if you have it. Light the kindling and place it inside the lower hole until the flame reaches the vertical hole.

Then, through the hole at the top drop small pieces of kindling to keep the fire going. It will not be long before an intense flame starts to emerge from the top of the log. If you now want to place a kettle on it, place three or four stones to allow a gap between under the kettle otherwise the fire will, of course, go out.

4 | A Wood of Your Own

REMEMBER THAT IN order to burn wood you must first fell a tree. There is no way round it. No tree, no firewood. It may have grown tall and stately over decades, but in order to feed your fire it will have to be brought down in just a few moments by the chainsaw's assault.

A forester is a man with a long gaze. He sees not weeks, months or even years ahead; his timescale is sometimes decades, but more likely it is centuries. He may spend his entire working life nurturing a tree that he will never see harvested, and just as likely he will fell one that first burst into life before his grandparents were born.

These profound thoughts may lead you to think that wood is far too precious to consider reducing to ash for your fleeting enjoyment, but think again. Woodlands and forests have lives that reflect our own; if no one died then we would populate ourselves to extinction, and only because a regular supply of us drop off the twig, so to speak, are the remainder allowed to flourish. So it is with woodlands. The foresters with their brutal and determined axes are keeping our woodlands alive and prospering, so have no fear that this natural resource is being terminally harmed by flinging it on the fire. Making woodland productive is the best guarantee of its survival and longevity.

There is much woodland that flashes past as you drive the rural roads and lanes that is hardly worthy of the name. To be a proper wood is to be a properly cultivated piece of land, as carefully tended as any agricultural field, and not a ragbag of bush, brash and

A dream to own, but hard work to manage – a wood of your own.

spindly trees. It is depressing to see woodland that nobody cares for. The romantic will coo at the sight of it, declaring it 'gloriously untouched', but there's nothing venerable about a neglected gathering of trees. They are smothering themselves by their own closeness, and they need our careful and planned intervention to make them not only productive but also sustaining. Woodland that has been left to its own devices creates a generation of trees that are untutored and wild, like unschooled children.

This is not how forests once were. A working wood was a resource, a productive area, a piece of land as giving as any farmer's field. The forest provided for those who worked and lived there, and they took their pleasure in them by hunting not just for sport but for food.

A skillful woodman knows that a forest that is flourishing in all its aspects is a healthy and productive place, and that he need have no reservations about taking timber from it. The modern woodman has the widest of visions and can see the complex interaction of all the elements that go to make up a wood, seeing far more than you and I will ever spot as we walk the dog or take a stroll. So don't fear the

'A HOUSE IS NOT A HOME UNLESS IT
CONTAINS FOOD AND FIRE FOR THE MIND
AS WELL AS THE BODY.'

BENJAMIN FRANKLIN

sound of the chainsaw for, although in the wrong hands it can do the most appalling damage, in the hands of those who truly understand the workings of the forest it can be the tree's greatest friend.

This idea that good woodland is managed woodland is stated with great force by the distinguished biologist and historian of the countryside, Oliver Rackham. In his definitive work, *Trees and Woodland in the British Landscape*, he writes, 'A huge inverted pyramid of argument has been built on the belief that trees die when cut down – a factoid which flatly denies the whole basis of woodmanship as practised over the last 500 years.' It does not take much consideration before you have to agree strongly with that sentiment; those unthinking country walkers who take to task a woodman going about his work should remember this before condemning him. Every forest worker I have met has, at one time or another, been branded a vandal by a thoughtless passer-by. As if the forester didn't have enough natural struggles to contend with, there's always the self-appointed conservationist, putting sentiment before understanding, who weeps, 'But all that *habitat* is being destroyed!'

But forests have always been going to waste in one way or another. The wind and winter kills trees and always will, but the diversity survives. Falling trees kill standing trees, and always will. Nature is not naturally kind to trees. But the forester is. He can get to the sick ones and bring them down cleanly so they can do no harm. Unlike the blinkered intensive farmer who seeks to exploit every scrap of land for maximum gain, the forester is in it for the long game and knows that the removal of one tree will allow air and light to enhance a neighbouring one, and so doesn't hesitate to bring a weakling down to allow others to flourish. The fact that the

Ash dieback disease is devastating ash trees across the country, eventually depriving us of the very best wood for burning.

tree he has nurtured may not itself be felled till he is long dead does not cross his mind; he knows that growing trees is not a business for anyone who enjoys a quick, profitable gain.

I have met a variety of foresters in rich and varied settings, and they all share a deep love of the places in which they work. I have met no vandals, nor opportunists. I have seen them torture themselves at the thought of cutting down a much-loved tree, which they know, in their hearts, must be removed. For them, it is like chopping out an old friend. I have seen them leave inconveniently located dead trees, which would be better removed, because they are home to bats and the myriads of other creatures which pass most of their lives unseen by us. I have seen them weep at the deathly damage done by marauding deer, and the idle but greedy muntjac who use their nasty tusks to idly strip a tree of its bark, condemning it to death, before moving on to the next. These creatures do more damage than any forester ever has. I have seen disconsolate looks on countless foresters' faces when yet another glorious ash tree shows signs of the terminal ash dieback disease, or the crippling honey fungus.

As bystanders, we wander the pathways, kicking the grass, feeling the bark of a passing tree, hearing the skylark hovering above a nearby field, and are completely unaware of the endless struggles played out in what we think of as being a place of peace and tranquility. And that is probably the way the forest prefers it. That it is a continuous battlefield is the forest's dark secret.

THE HISTORY OF WOODLANDS

If we exclude the trees planted for scenic effect, and those left to grow in hedgerows, the ones we see largely fall into two categories. There are woodland trees which have appeared naturally, and there are plantation trees which have been put there – it's as simple as that. Woodlands of naturally occurring trees can be managed using the skills of woodmanship, and those that were there centuries ago can also be managed to be productive while remaining undiminished. But this requires fine judgement. The woodman needs to take timber from his woodland while leaving just enough to allow the wood to prosper down the ages. As far as the plantations are concerned, it is more of a farming operation, in which a crop is planted, harvested and that's it. Woodmen are in it for the long term, tree farmers for the quick buck. We'll ignore the plantations, for this is not where our firewood will come from.

A bit of history. When the ice age came to an end, about 12,000 years ago, Britain was a bleak spot. It's landscape was Siberian in appearance, cold and barren frozen moorland. With no cultivated land or farmland to get in their way, trees slowly began to appear, reproduce and spread. This created the 'wildwoods' of hazel, ash, elm, alder and pine. Which species predominated depended on location and ground type. Despite the reverence given to the sturdy oak tree, Rackham notes that of all the trees that made up the wildwood, oak may have be the scarcest and their appearance should be considered 'recent'.

If much of England was originally covered by wildwood after the ice age retreat, then by 500 BC half of it had gone, that loss accelerating during the Iron Age when better axes superseded flints and the plough began to be developed. Agriculture was by now on the march. By the time of the Domesday Book (1086) there was probably no wildwood left in England. The techniques of coppicing were now widely used and woodland had become a mixture of what we call 'standards', or tall trees, and coppiced undergrowth which would have supplied firewood and fencing. The standards would have been selectively felled to feed the increasing appetite for timber in building or ship construction, for which the most desirable wood was oak. The first sawmills, introduced into England in 1633 by Germans, were destroyed by foresters who feared for their jobs – early Luddites.

What changed wildwood into the woodland that we recognise today was the breaking up of these once vast areas of trees into smaller parcels as cultivation advanced. Once broken down into individual patches these woods were given names and identities, people took ownership of them and these owners created boundaries, defining the woods even further. Seeking to make their woodlands productive, differing management techniques evolved, one of the more important being fencing to prevent incursion by deer, sheep or goats, which lazily eat the fresh young shoots of anything that emerges from the ground.

Coppicing, the art of cutting back trees without killing them and allowing them to regrow, has been traced back to Neolithic times, but by the beginning of the twentieth century had almost ceased. Coal may have been to blame, for the expanding railways brought this cheap fuel to the towns and then even to the smaller villages. Coppicing had traditionally provided wood for charcoal, used in the production of steel, but coke was replacing it. When we needed wood to make paper and other products requiring cellulose, we imported it, until the First World War intervened and the government of the day then decided on a policy of planting vast swathes of conifers still seen today, but which cannot be coppiced – cut down a conifer and it's dead. The pine forests that march across our upland and moorland areas are not really forests at all; they are tree farms.

The middle part of the twentieth century was a bad time for the ancient woodlands, which are understood to mean areas of wood

The planted pine forests of the early twentieth century – tree farms, really.

that existed in 1600 before planting occurred, and can therefore be assumed to have developed naturally. By 1975, according to Rackham, nearly half of the ancient woodland had been destroyed over a thirty-year period. Ancient forests were thought of as valueless to landowners and inconvenient to farmers, an attitude encouraged by governments who saw them as a 'waste'. These were the years when the destructive diggers flung aside the ancient roots, and the unthinking army of planters who gave us those grim vistas of dreary, and eventually uneconomic, conifers so densely packed that no light penetrates and nothing flourishes beneath their canopy. Nothing sums up better our financial impatience and our arrogance than what we did to our forests in the twentieth century.

Times and attitudes change, and our woodlands are valued once again, if often romantically and without any deep understanding of how they work nor any true sense of their value in the natural cycle of affairs. Coppicers are at work again. If carbon fuel prices increase, then heating with wood becomes attractive and the skills of the coppicer will be in demand once more. Like a predator, though, governments can easily screw things up by introducing planting schemes not thought through, bringing short-termism to a process that must be planned over centuries and not as far ahead as the next election. Growing trees is not a tidy, nor a linear business, which makes accountants sceptical. Even the Great Storm of October 1987 was judged publicly to be a disaster for the tree population. But it was not as big a disaster, Rackham notes, as the panic that set in immediately after the event, when battalions of men had been sent in to 'tidy up the forests' armed with a battery of screeching chainsaws; Rackham claims far more damage was done by their intrusions than had been wreaked by the wind. Some months after the hurricane, when the next growing season came round, it transpired that most of the trees which had been thought to have been killed in the storm were, in fact, alive and bursting into new growth. Nature is very good at showing two fingers to those who think they know more about her ways than she does.

It is hard for an appreciation of the slow and mysterious ways of the forest to find a place in an increasingly knee-jerk world. To get a real understanding, I went for a walk in the woods.

In fact, I visited several woods to meet the modern breed of woodland owner. Each tended their trees for different reasons, but all shared a deep love of the forest or woodland they owned, and understood its value and precious nature. These are the men (there are few women foresters) who will feed our fires, but not destroy our landscape in doing so. Their woods will be as productive in a hundred years time as they are today, for they know that they are only temporary custodians and their trees will still be flourishing when they are long gone.

THE MODERN WOODSMAN: CRISPIN CHALKER

Crispin loves his wood deeply. It is a true affair of the heart. It is close to where I have lived for the best part of forty years, yet shamefully I never noticed it nor gave it a second thought. I suppose I could not see the woodland for the trees.

Goodness knows the number of times I have sped up the A-road that follows the old Roman road from London to Colchester, and then onwards through Suffolk to my home. A map from 1776, when the supposedly mad King George III was on the throne, shows pretty much the same route as today, though this road will surely have been there long before that. It snakes through none of the great forests of the south-east, but skirts countless patches of woodland which in my county, Suffolk, are in abundance. In fact, so common are small patches of woodland that they squat peacefully on the landscape, part of the furniture, an unchanging constituent of the scenery, easily ignored.

Crispin's is another of those woods to which you'd never give a second glance. It is reached by a track so narrow that you wouldn't spot that either. This wood was certainly here in the time of George III, and who can guess how many years before that? Local records believe it to have been part of the Manor of the Sowters, without revealing who they were. Crispin says there is evidence of a moat, if you look hard enough and use your imagination, suggesting a manor house. There are signs, too, of an old stockman's house, and Green Hellebore has been found, a plant which had medicinal properties when used to treat cattle but is toxic to humans and grew well in beech forests. This was clearly once a place of humans as well as trees, and we can only imagine it once formed an area where trees and grazing animals lived side by side – 'wood-pasture', this is called.

This secretive patch of woodland sits on the brow of a rising piece of land, rare hereabouts in a fairly flat landscape, and in a commanding position looking down on the ceaseless traffic.

Here I met Crispin Chalker, one of a new generation of foresters who has balanced an overpowering ambition to own a forest with the need to make some money from it. The previous owner was the exact opposite: an unthinking timber merchant who bought the 50-acre patch, removed from it standing trees of any commercial value, and left it heartless for years. Without careful tending it had become tall and straggly – 'overstood' is the forester's description. Crispin is setting about reversing that in a compassionate way that a previous ownership would have thought unnecessary. As we sit over a wood fire in a converted workman's van, in his engaging way he tells me the story.

'I never had a burning ambition to own a wood, it just sort of grew. But I've always felt a connection with woods. I'd done a bit of tree surgery in my time, but that's just about it. My mother died, I had a bit of money, and this wood came up for sale. I came to see it. I thought, 'My God!' I never knew this was here. The buying of it was one of those competitions where you had to put in a sealed

PLAYING WITH FIRE

bid and I had no idea what would happen, so we bunged in a figure. Anyway, the phone went one day and the voice of the estate agent on the other end said, 'You're now the owner of a woodland.' And I can remember standing there on the drive with a tingling feeling. I was simply ecstatic. People said I was insane. Of course, I hadn't got a clue what to do, but I knew I was going to have to use the wood to create income so I decided to go into the firewood business. I soon found out that you're quite restricted in what you can do. You can't just go lopping down trees. You have to apply for licences, and so on. I honestly didn't know what I was doing when I started out ten years ago.'

'The first thing I did was get people together,' he explains. 'I knew things had to be done. I knew it was the sort of land that got very sodden when it was wet and if you start using heavy machinery you're going to do damage that will take years to recover. This had been a problem in years gone by because I did find evidence of some early lattice drainage work so someone had tried to tackle the drainage years back. Then there were the deer, and they were a real problem. I knew the wood was in severe decline. I could see it. They said it had been thinned but, in fact, it has been raided. There are lots of woods around that are completely unmanaged, and that's a shame, but it's better than robbing them of everything they're worth.'

An approach emerged, and not one an accountant would have recognised.

'I decided I was going to fit in as sympathetically as I could. I couldn't look at my wood and see it as a gang of individual trees. It's a living, breathing thing. The wood comes first, and I do my utmost to tilt every decision I make in the direction of the wood. The woodland must come first, it has to.

'I often sit here and think of all the people who've worked in this wood over the years, and the knowledge they had. That has now all gone. I'd love to have been a fly on the wall and listen to those old woodmen. They'd probably have lived and worked here all their lives, and there's no substitute for that.

'If I have an ambition, it is to do what they did back then, and justify every bit of wood I remove from here. They used to make so many things, use every scrap of timber, and firewood was at the bottom of the pile. There's so much you can do with wood, so much potential. But most of the traditional uses for wood have gone, and firewood's at the top of my list now. It has to be. But that doesn't mean I don't understand the value of it. I think about it all the time I'm slicing up a seventy-year-old tree.'

He laughs.

'I'm not certain the firewood customers do, though. If I deliver some wood and the customer says 'that last load was lovely, burnt a treat' it puts wind in my sails. It's really good. But I'm not certain many of them do appreciate it, and I find those hard to deal with. They don't care about it, just fling it on the fire.'

Like all good woodmen, Crispin takes his love of wood, and fires, all the way through to his own hearth.

'I'm a confessed pyromaniac. We've always got a wood fire at home and I can sit round it for hours. There's something about embers. Yes, very special are embers. And I can feel awful if I've tried to light a fire and it hasn't taken …'

The kettle starts to sing and Crispin pours more tea. I feel I have met someone with a true understanding of what it is to own a wood. He is far from a sentimentalist, though. He has worked out for himself the striking of a balance between his need for a living, and his ambition not only to keep his wood alive but restore it to his youthful vigour. He has owned his wood for only a decade, but to hear him speak with passion and the benefit of experience, you could believe he had been there all his life.

Perhaps those old woodmen are still talking to him, for he speaks a language they would have understood.

Crispin wisely took the advice of others more experienced that himself. One of the first people he turned to was Pete Fordham, an experienced woodsman and a more knowledgeable man you couldn't wish to meet. He has had in his care for over forty years a precious parcel of 200 acres of land near Bury St Edmunds called Bradfield Woods, described by the late Oliver Rackham as 'a place of wonder and delight'.

Now administered by the Suffolk Wildlife Trust, these woods appear to have everything a woodland could possibly want. The trees apart, this is a place of yellow oxlips and orchids, and a rich variety of evil-named fungi, such as ink cap and bright red fly

Pete Fordham
– a woodsman
for forty years.

agaric, which seep out of the ground when the trees are thinned in the winter. These are just two species of fungi found in Bradfield Woods not found anywhere else in Britain. Over 300 species of trees and plants have been catalogued, this largely due to the complexity and variety of the soils. But the most spectacular and most unmissable of all are the ash stools, remnants of generations of

Ancient ash stools in Bradfield Woods – the oldest living things in the east of England.

coppicing which reveal where the older growth has been removed, and where the new growth sprouts. Coppicing here dates back to 1252 when Henry III was on the throne. In that year the king received from the people of Norway the gift of a polar bear, which His Majesty allowed to swim in the River Thames.

Kings come and go but ash stools seem eternal and to come across them, as you frequently do as you wander this wood, is a spiritual moment. It is the considered view of experts that these ash stools might well be the oldest living things in this part of the world and it is tempting, as you gaze down at them, to bow your head in respect.

But instead, turn your head high in the spring and you will hear the nightingale, of which there is a decent population, then look downwards to watch the field mouse scurrying about its work. Taken as a whole, this is ancient woodland at its finest.

Bradfield is not just a wood to wonder at, it is a working place producing firewood, fencing stakes, hazel rods for growing beans and peas, and ash poles for all manner of garden uses. Until recent years, a local factory bought wood from here to make garden rakes, scythe handles and other gardening tools.

'I first came here in 1981,' Pete Fordham remembers as he approaches the final few months before his retirement, although few doubt he will turn his back on this place completely. It has been his canvas where he has practised the woodman's craft for over forty years, and he probably knows more secrets of this forest than anyone has ever been able to record.

'I remember when I first started here I was doing some coppicing, cutting trees back and so on. And someone came up to me and said, "Oh, what are you going to plant in its place?" They didn't realise that the trees would all grow back on their own!

'What I like about this place is that it's a working wood, and people who come here like it that way too. We bring in an income, and I love that. But it's a lot of work, especially with the firewood. We first have to fell it, then cut it in to lengths and we're doing that for about four months of the year. We can't start till November because of the door mice. And then we're very busy. Four months to cut and coppice eight or nine acres a year. We cut the hazel first, then the bigger stuff such as the ash, willow, alder and birch, and then we start to extract it between April and June and then stack it in an outside barn. Yes, it's a lot of work but it's bringing in the best part of £40,000 a year. But we're not working this wood for profit, of course; the nature comes first.'

To achieve that balance requires a well thought out management plan.

'It needs very careful looking after, this wood. For example the brambles can close over the ground and then we'd lose some of our unique flora. There's bettany, bluebells, wood anemones, wood spurge – we could lose all that. And then there's the deer, we've got to try and keep them out as well. Ash die back is a real problem for us now. I've seen newly sprouting ash which has been dead in three years. That's very sad when you think some of our giant ash stools have been here over 500 years.

'Most of the customers are wood stove owners. I only sell within a 4-mile radius. Some of them ask for a particular wood, not many, but I tell them I can't separate it. I sell it when it's six months after cutting, but I always tell people it needs to be stacked longer than

Modern machinery meets ancient woodland in Bradfield Woods, Suffolk.

that, so I suggest they store it for another year and use it then. A lot of them have got some learning to do about burning wood. I ask them if they burn it on an open grate and they tell me how they clean it out every day because it 'looks untidy otherwise'. Of course, that's the wrong thing to do; wood burns best on a bed of its own ash. And some of the tree surgeons, for whom selling firewood is a bit of a sideline, they won't promise you how dry their wood is.'

And then he reflects.

'I still love it. I love this place. I like seeing it through all the seasons, especially the late spring and early summer. And I'll miss the nightingales when I leave.'

At which point Pete Fordham returns to the tractor-driven machine that cuts and splits his coppiced trees into hunks of wood ready for drying then burning. The woodmen come and go in Bradfield Woods, and Peter Fordham has been reckoned a giant amongst them. Meanwhile, the ancient ash stools sit silently on the floor of this wood and watch the years pass by.

You might get the impression, listening to the passion with which Pete Fordham speaks, and the commitment that Crispin Chalker shows, that every bit of woodland in Britain hsd such dedicated guardians. While it might be true of places like Bradfield, which comes under the safe umbrella of a dedicated conservation group, you do not have to stroll far off the beaten track to come across a wood that has no one to care for it. There is a very different picture to paint regarding the health of our woodland which I gleaned from Simon Lloyd, the director of the RFS, the Royal Forestry Society, which has 3,500 members and is an educational charity promoting woodland management.

'We haven't got enough foresters and we've just been through a difficult patch. Prices collapsed in the 1990s and it was difficult to make any money out of woodland. And the age profile of people involved in forestry became skewed towards older people. The result is that, as they retire, we are being faced with a real skills crisis.

'The trouble is that forestry is undervalued by the government. It falls between two stools – agriculture and conservation. And it's overwhelmed by bureaucracy. It's a massive missed opportunity but its contribution isn't valued. As a result, 60 per cent of the trees in Britain are not managed, and that's 60 to 100 million tons of hardwood that could come to the market, but isn't. We are only harvesting 14 per cent of our annual growth, but still importing 80 per cent of our timber. Did you know that if you pick up logs at a garage, 50 per cent of them will be imported timber? It's true we've seen an increase in demand for firewood, and woodchip has helped to bring some woods into management, but that's usually short rotation willow. It's really the lowest-quality stuff, and woodchip is the lowest-quality forest product. But it at least gives a floor to the market. But firewood, in economic terms, remains a small business. Still, ten years ago some people were having to pay to have firewood taken away. At least that's changed.'

Simon Lloyd's own interest in forestry started back in the days of Dutch elm disease in the late 1960s when a particularly virulent strain of the disease spread from Europe to cause devastation to standing elms killing 25 million trees in the UK.

'My family had some woods in Herefordshire, about 50 acres around a farm. I decided to do a second degree, which was quite a struggle in certain respects because there's quite a lot of biology, maths and chemistry. It was the biology that I found tricky. But the attraction of doing it was having a career that took me outside – as simple as that. I've learnt a lot and made a hell of a lot of mistakes, and at times it's heartbreaking. I lost a huge amount of 10-year-old oak to squirrels; they just ring-barked the trees and that was that. I've learned about squirrel control since. Then I harvested some mature conifers so I could put back some broad-leafed trees and I foolishly used short rabbit guards to save some money. I should have used full-length tubes. You can't be a cheapskate if you're running a wood. You've got to invest the time and money. Woods don't look after themselves, and woods shouldn't be left alone. It's part of the message that we try to spread through our members, that woods are working places. We encourage woodland workers to talk to walkers and explain what they're doing. Our licence to operate comes from the public, really.'

He has two wood stoves, fuelled by his own timber. 'There's joy in a wood fire, it's a focus for your attention. I like the whole experience of producing wood and I know and recognise each piece of it that I throw on the fire. It is a complete process, and one to be enjoyed.'

If a dark cloud hangs heavy over much of our woodland, there is at least one in the midst of East Anglia where the light is beginning to shine. One small village has embraced a 22-acre patch of woodland and is starting to think of it as its own. This is all thatnks to David Mitchell, whose mother died young and left him the money to purchase a patch of woodland which had been so devastated by the 1987 hurricane that is was impossible to gain access. Now it is emerging as a community woodland where the locals exchange their labour for loads of firewood, and where schools encourage children to learn to use bow saws and the techniques of coppicing. All the generations are joining in here, which is important because Mitchell may have come up with the answer to the abiding question of what to do with our neglected woodlands, often left to grow wild

David Mitchell, head over heels in his community woodland.

by farmers who show no interest or can see no way of making even a small profit.

'I did this because I wanted to do something that meant something. The previous owner had taken out most of the standard trees and replanted it in the 1950s. But there were a handful of big trees left and I asked him why? He said it was a Friday afternoon and he couldn't be bothered and went home! Then he applied for permission to turn it into a caravan site and that was turned down, and that's how I got it.

'My first job was to start clearing the rides, the pathways, to get good access. The only tools I had were an old Fergie tractor, a chainsaw and a wife. I used to finish work, and I had a full-time job and it was hard, and then together we'd come into here and we'd be here till nine at night.

'I could have gone down the short-term felling route, and just taken as much out of here as I could, but I didn't want to do that. I wanted a plan for the whole wood. And what I tried to do was dovetail all the romantic ideas of owning a wood with all the professional advice I could gather. But it was all about the wood. I knew as soon as I got it that I wanted to prove something to a world that doesn't care. You need two things: a management plan and a vision. Of course, a lot of people think you shouldn't cut a thing down but I knew that wasn't right, so I spent two whole years tapping the knowledge of experts.'

But the world, or at least that bit of it close to David's wood, did start to care when they saw the progress he was making after eight years of hard work, clearing rides and getting access to the interior of the wood, careful to avoid any discarded Second World War munitions which might have been dumped from the nearby wartime air base.

'People started to get interested, so I built on that. There were all sorts of people; there was a man from the Prudential, a landscape architect, a retired lecturer. They come and they go. I give them some practical advice, they get access to the machinery, and they get wood in return.

'What I want to end up with is a productive woodland that's commercial, has some value to the ecology, and is part of the community. And I'm getting there. I'm getting close to it. What I'm doing now is maintaining a guiding hand. I've got a plan that goes to 2021 and my objective is to plan for resilience. That's important. We've got diseases, like ash dieback, and we've got climate change, and a changing economy, and I'm trying to insulate the wood from all those things.

'I still get a thrill from selling the wood. I sell it to local pubs and I don't need to advertise because people go in for a drink, see a blazing fire, and ask where the wood came from. I can deliver one load of good wood to a pub and get half a dozen new customers straight away. I shift about 90 tons a year and that's a sustainable amount for a wood of this size.

'There's a lot of satisfaction over a broad front. I've got schools coming in and the kids help build deer fences. It's especially good for kids who are having a hard time at school, or perhaps they've got health problems. I teach them about the economy of the woodland too, how you've got to sell wood to keep it going. Yes, there's satisfaction on a broad front.

'For me, three things need to come together: the economy of the wood, the ecology of the place and the social side of a community wood. And I'm getting there, I'm really getting there.'

David Mitchell may prove to be well ahead of his time, for councils and local authorities are trying to tie together lots of lose ends by encouraging people to think about how they can use less energy and to consider renewable resources – such as burning wood instead of consuming oil. A council officer, John Taylor, charged with getting across this broad message told me, 'There's a cultural disconnect between communities and their local woodlands and we are trying to make that connection work. It's strange that we make maximum use of every scrap of farmland but don't get the best out of woodlands and forests. In a way, it's like going back to the "good life" initiatives of the 1970s, except this time it's about reconnecting with landscape. But in the end it comes down to personalities to make it work. Someone's got to take the initiative. But in this age of social media, it ought to be easier to get that message across than ever before.'

As if to prove that personality is what it takes for community woodland to thrive, you need only see the grin of satisfaction on David Mitchell's face as he walks you round his woodland with the confidence of a man who knows that a very important experiment is taking place here.

Coppicing a Hornbeam. The stools will regrow for the next generation to take a harvest of wood.

MANAGING WOODLAND FOR FIREWOOD

Within any woodland there will be mature, standard trees which will need to be felled. They may have become dangerous, inconveniently placed, or are causing too much shade which prevents the underwood from flourishing. They may have stood for a century but the woodman has to harden his heart and cut them out. These, however, should not be your prime source of firewood.

Coppicing is one of those techniques which seems almost too good to be true. By removing wood, you create more wood – magic, isn't it? Cut the tree back to a stump (except conifers which don't coppice) and within a few years you will have more standing timber than you had before. How long it takes will depend on the species; oak may take fifty years, ash or willow might provide useful wood in under ten. Regrowth will start in the first year with shoots bursting from the stumps (known as 'stools') and these new shoots will fatten as the years go by. Not only that, but in the fullness of

PLAYING WITH FIRE

It looks brutal but this ensures a tree will have a life for centuries to come.

time when you coppice again, the stools will burst into life once more and deliver yet another harvest. This can go on for centuries. Ash stools in particular live to very ripe old ages, maybe hundreds of year.

The trick is quite a simple one, and if it could be adapted to mankind we would be laughing (perhaps) because what you are doing to a tree when you coppice it is to prevent it from ever getting old. Just at that stage in its life when it is getting fat round the belly, along you come and cut it back right down to its toes. It then sprouts again with the vigour of a youngster. The shape of freshly sprouted stool is worth a second glance, for you'll see that the new growth curves somewhat outwards before reaching for the sky. It realises, of course, that it is going to have to compete for light and this is the way in which it gives itself some elbow room. Coppicing is of great benefit to species that inhabit woodland floors but need a bit of sunlight in order to flourish. Coppice woodland will typically be rich in primroses, anemones and

bluebells, and with consequent populations of birds, insects and butterflies ancient coppiced woodland can be the most species-rich of any woodland.

They worked this out in the depths of pre-history, and exactly the same techniques are being used today and are being modified to meet modern demands. Short rotation coppice is grown to provide energy in a system widely used in Sweden where high-yielding poplar and willow are cut on as little as a three-year cycle, the wood providing biomass which is in turn burnt in power stations.

For proper management, a woodland needs to be divided into areas known as 'coupes', which are based on the size of the whole plot, but plan for each coupe to be coppiced only once every ten years. If the majority of the wood is faster growing alder, poplar or willow then less than ten years might be a better timescale. In the UK, you do not need a felling licence if the coppice poles are no larger than 15cm in diameter at your chest height, 1.3m above the ground.

The harvest ready for splitting, chopping and stacking

If you are working your wood only for your own use, the accepted statistic is that to fully heat a three-bedroomed house with wood, you will consume between 7 and 10 tons of dry wood a year. To produce this from coppiced woodland would require an area of at least 3 hectares. Traditionally, though, coppicing provided much more than firewood. It was the source of raw materials for charcoal making which was essential to the iron-smelting process, and fence poles, walking sticks, poles to act as crop supports and wood for hurdles.

The coppicing season starts in the autumn after leaf fall and lasts throughout the winter.

The sixteenth-century writer and diarist John Evelyn gave coppicing advice in his *Sylva, or a Discourse of Forest-Trees and the Propagation of Timber*, which was presented as a paper to the Royal Society in 1662. This book was the first ever close analysis of the English countryside and was widely read outside academic circles. Landowners were inspired by it and responded to Evelyn's pleas for them to plant more trees. Much of its advice remains good to this day:

> The underwood may be cut from January, at the latest, till mid-March or April; or from mid-September, till near the end of November.

Unless the coppice is quite mature, you will have no need of a chainsaw and a bow saw will serve just as well. Young coppice can be felled with a billhook, although this requires more experience to get a clean cut. The cut should be made at an angle, designed to prevent water gathering and leading to rot. If you are going to create a slope, have it facing south for warmth and faster drying.

> Cut not above half a foot from the ground, nay the closer, the better, and that to the south, slopewise.

Once felled, the timber can then be cut to suitable length for easy transport, usually by hand if doing it on a small scale. The wood can then be stacked and allowed to dry.

The stools must now be protected as there are many enemies, mostly deer, muntjac and rabbits for whom the new spring shoots provide a tasty salad bar after bleak winter rations.

If you can exclude all animals by fencing then that is clearly the best way, if the most expensive. A fence 6–8ft high is needed to keep out a determined deer.

A cheaper, though less certain method, is to cover the stools with brash and trimmings taken from the branches after felling. This would, in times past, have been bundled into faggots, but no longer. Although time-expensive, brash can be built into a stout barrier which will deter, but not completely exclude, deer.

Electric fencing can be effective against deer. So can culling, if carried out within the law and by experienced marksmen.

Coppicing has gone on as long as we have been creating woodlands, and it should be approached with the greatest respect. It is not random slashing and culling, but a measured approach to the production of firewood which is totally and miraculously self-repairing. You are taking part in small miracle without which

A properly run wood allows nothing to go to waste

mankind may have starved to death many thousands of years ago.

It is a mistake to be too tidy in running a wood. Dead trees may litter the ground, rotting and lifeless, but someone appreciates them. Look carefully to see holes where dormice might live. Behind loose bark there will be creepers and insects; woodpeckers dig for food in the rotting wood at the ends of branches; bats will roost in standing trees; insects will gorge on juices from ivy.

In life or in death, the tree never stops giving.

A variety of woods, drying in the autumn sun, ready to burn in the coming winter.

5 | Wood to Burn

FIREWOOD – 'THE POOR MAN'S CLOAK'

IT IS AUTUMN, I can feel it in my bones. It is not a moment too soon for the winter logs to have arrived, noisily dumped outside the house in an unruly pile, pleading for a willing pair of hands to wheelbarrow them to the kind of shelter they enjoyed under the forest canopy. They do not naturally belong in the brightness of the day. Your logs may have spent two years (if you're lucky) ridding themselves of moisture, being wafted by drying breezes, making ready to blaze, and you can risk it all by letting October rains drown the life out of them. So get them under cover and keep the damp away. How to stack your logs to guarantee a blazing winter we shall come to later, but for the moment, before you so much as shift the first lump of wood, we need to look at that pile of wood, and in some detail.

Unless you have an expert eye, you will not be able to tell one log from another. Pine might stick out amongst the rest, but more for its scent that its appearance. Beech can often be spotted by its smooth bark, but there again it might be hornbeam, or am I thinking of sycamore? And if you ask your log merchant, 'What's in here?' you are guaranteed a vague reply, and not because he's trying to cheat you but because he might not know either. They will have come from a pile that was cut over months and stacked over weeks, possibly years ago. Only an expert woodsman would be able to identify each log as if it were his own.

All woods burn, but some burn better than others.

However, you really need to know what's in that pile. It will determine if you are going to spend the winter reaching for one sweater or two on cold nights. The burning properties of wood are as varied as the differing tastes of the loaves on a baker's shelf. Some wood will smoulder and spit, while others will blaze gloriously and noisily away, but not for long, like a cheery friend that breezes in and out. There are certain things you demand from a piece of burning wood: you need heat, certainly, but some flame to go with it. Add to the list the scent of burning wood, almost as invigorating as the flames themselves. Then there are things you don't want; some wood has a habit of spitting at you as if it really dislikes keeping you warm. Add all these requirements together and you find that it is almost impossible to put a name to the perfect burning wood.

And another thought. This is a major turning point in the life of the wood when certain facts have to be faced. Your firewood has not made it into the super league, it hasn't won the beauty contest and been sculpted into desirable furniture. It has been judged not even to be worthy of use in the building trade. It really is at the bottom of the woodpile. Your logs are a failure, fit for nothing more

PLAYING WITH FIRE

than flinging on the fire. But that is no reason to disrespect them. We know, of course, that a log's true glory is yet to shine out, but for the moment it lies broken. But to generations past it was a bringer of good fortune, a medicine to cure ills, a charm to warn off demons. You can ignore this as being fanciful if you wish, but a full enjoyment of a fire demands a full understanding of what wood stands for, why it is one of the most remarkable things that grows on the planet, and its place in our long evolving culture. Let all this history play out across your ceiling when you dim the harsh electric light and let the glow of the embers fill your room.

I am certainly not going to tell you which wood is best for burning; it would be as presumptuous as advising you which colour to wear. All I can do is list the most common woods that you might be offered, be honest about their virtues and their failings, and for the full enjoyment of those flickering embers I will add a little of their history and character.

To be ruthlessly scientific about it, though, you can take some of the various woods and measure the heat each one gives off:

WOOD	MILLIONS OF BTUS PER CORD (APPROX)
Oak	29
Beech	28
Apple	27
Birch	26
Maple	25
Walnut	23
Juniper	22
Birch	21
Douglas Fir	21
Cherry	20
Ash	20
Elm	20
Sycamore	19
Chestnut	17
Willow	17
Alder	17
Pine	16
Spruce	15

A British thermal unit (BTU) is a standard measurement for heat sources and is the amount of energy required to raise the temperature of 1lb of water by 1°F – very imperial. In the above list, the figures given are for a cord of wood, which is defined as 128 cu.ft, or 8 x 4 x 4ft. This is not to be confused with the loose term 'a load of firewood', which no one has been able to define, not least the person who is selling it to you.

Taking the above figures at face value, it would appear as if the best choice is oak, while pine does pretty badly down the bottom end of the scale. But anyone who has burnt oak will know it has a tendency to burn only slowly, taking a while to get going, whereas pine leaps into life and while it may not last long it will give you a quick heat. That doesn't make pine inferior, just different. In fact, the secret of a good fire might well be in the making of a cocktail where the hasty pine gets the fire going while the slow, old oak comes along later to give off its vast store of heat.

The hardness of woods must be considered, and it is a fact that if you compare wood not by volume but by weight, all woods would produce pretty much the same heat. It is simply that your cord of oak weighs far more than your pine and there is consequently more energy in it. In fact, a cord of good, dry hardwood has the energy equivalent of burning 200 gallons of oil. Unless you want frequent trips to the woodpile, a dense hardwood would seem to be the better choice.

It is a broad truth that hardwood is better than softwood. Because softwood is less dense you will need more of it to create the same amount of heat.

Having seen what science has to offer, perhaps poetry can give us a greater insight.

This is a traditional rhyme, and the advice given in the first verse is as relevant today as when it was first written:

Logs to burn, logs to burn,
Logs to save the coal a turn.
Here's a word to make you wise,
When you hear the woodman's cries.
Never heed his usual tale,
That he has good logs for sale.
But read these lines and really learn,
The proper kind of logs to burn.

OAK logs will warm you well,
If they're old and dry.
LARCH logs of pine wood smell,
But the sparks will fly.
BEECH logs for Christmas time,
YEW logs heat well.
SCOTCH logs it is a crime,
For anyone to sell.
BIRCH logs will burn too fast,
CHESTNUT scarce at all.
HAWTHORN logs are good to last,
If you cut them in the fall.
HOLLY logs will burn like wax,
You should burn them green.
ELM logs like smouldering flax,
No flame to be seen
PEAR logs and APPLE logs,
they will scent your room.
CHERRY logs across the dogs,
Smell like flowers in bloom.
But ASH logs, all smooth and grey,
burn them green or old;
Buy up all that come your way,
They're worth their weight in gold.

And with similar advice:

> Beechwood logs burn bright and clear,
> If the wood is kept a year.
> Store your beech for Christmas-tide,
> With new-cut holly laid aside.
> Chestnut's only good they say
> If for years it's stored away.
> Birch and Fir wood burn too fast,
> Blaze too bright, and do not last
> Flames from larch will shoot up high,
> And dangerously the sparks will fly.
> But ash wood green,
> And ash wood brown
> Are fit for Queen with golden crown.
>
> Oaken logs, if dry and old
> Keep away the winters cold
> Poplar gives a bitter smoke
> Fills your eyes and makes you choke
> Elmwood burns like churchyard mould
> Even the very flames burn cold
> Hawthorn bakes the sweetest bread
> So it is in Ireland said
> Applewood will scent the room
> Pears wood smells like a flower in bloom
> But ash wood wet and ash wood dry
> A King may warm his slippers by.

Be you king or queen, nothing would seem to better the burning properties of ash.

WOOD FOR BURNING (ALPHABETICALLY)

ALDER

This is slow-burning stuff, often found in wet, swampy areas, and a dull wood which burns quickly but produces little heat. Its saving grace is that it makes good charcoal. It is a soft wood, and because of its straight grain splits easily.

It is a soft and porous wood, likes marsh and boggy ground, and enjoys nothing more than being wet. Once dry, although no use for burning, it has found favour with boat builders, for building sluice gates for canals, and it was alder which provided the durable foundations for Venice. It has also found favour with makers of guitars where it is said to provide a 'balanced' tone. As the pith is easily pushed out of the green shoots, it can be made into whistles, making it the most musical of woods. Because of its liking for water, it was the wood of choice for clogs for those working in damp conditions.

When first cut, the wood turns a deep orange, as if it were bleeding. This led to the felling of it being banned in Ireland and it was certainly unlucky to pass one. Alder leaves slipped into your shoes are said to keep your feet cool.

APPLE

This is a well-behaved wood. It burns slowly and steadily, although the flame is small and doesn't spit. Because it gives good heat and little flame, it makes it an ideal wood for cooking.

The real joy of apple is in the scent it gives off when burning. The smoke smells sweetly delicious and it is a shame to waste it by letting it drift up the chimney. Smoke a ham in it, if you can.

Apple is such a lovely wood for turning and carving (though tough and hard work), and since an apple tree is only a small affair, it seems almost too good to put on the fire. If you decide to, the advice is to get it chopped while it is still green or it will be very difficult to split when dry.

ASH

This is one of the few woods which will burn when it is green – 'Ash, mature or green, makes a fire fit for a Queen' – but it is at its best when well seasoned when it will burn with a steady flame giving good heat and not much smoke. It will also ward off evil spirits. It has a naturally low moisture content, even when first cut, which gives it its green-burning reputation. More importantly, it will season that much faster. Because it is a largely knot-free wood, it can be easier to cut and split. It has a natural springiness and will absorb shocks without fracturing. It has been immensely useful in the making of tools, handles for hammers, shafts for carts, even hockey sticks. Oar makers are fond of it too, and it is good for the shafts of brooms.

Because it coppices well, it is a useful wood for both firewood and charcoal production.

The tall and delicate ash tree: one of the best to look at, and the best to burn.

The ash tree has strong mystical associations. To the Vikings it was the 'Tree of Life', and sometimes called 'The Venus of the Woods'. The leaves are said to attract prosperity and love, but you should not stand under an ash tree (or any other tree for that matter) as they are said to attract lightning.

The ash tree is a link between the gods, humans and those in the spirit world.

It is part of the olive family.

BEECH

Beech has a high water content, which means it can take longer to season than other woods. It also dries to a tough old lump and is better split when green. However, once dry it can burn as well as ash.

The words 'beech' and 'book' have similar roots and so the beech tree is known as the tree of knowledge, giving insight into the relationship between the past and the future. Beech was often used to provide a surface on which to write.

BIRCH

A hasty wood, which can be burnt unseasoned and will give you a lovely fire but not for long. It is perhaps best mixed with slower-burning hardwoods. However, the heat output is high, the flames have vigour and the scent is pleasing. The bark is thin and paper-like and thin sheets of it can be easily removed. These contain an oil which makes the birch bark useful for kindling a fire and is known as the 'camper's friend'. Don't let cut birch lie on the ground too long as it has a tendency to rot.

Also known as 'The Lady of the Woods', this is a wood associated with new beginnings, purification and fertility. The birch is a very useful tree: its sap was once a source of sugar, the inner bark can give pain relief, and the leaves can treat arthritis.

The silver birch – quick to burn, ubiquitous, and known as 'the camper's friend'.

BLACKTHORN

You won't find a decent-sized blackthorn log, but if you can get hold of any then you have a wood that burns with a good heat and a steady flame. Because it is often found as prunings from hedging work, the small pieces can be bundled to make excellent kindling. However, the fruit of the blackthorn tree is the sloe and lovers of sloe gin may prefer to leave it the grow and fruit in the hedgerow. It gives off little smoke. A drawback can be the nasty thorns; handle with gloves.

CHERRY

Like many of the orchard woods, cherry is a joy to burn. It is true that it is a slow burner, but it gives off good quantities of heat and has a glorious smell with which to fill the house at Christmas. It can spark a little.

Like apple and thorn tree wood, cherry will give you ample heat. Like a fine whiskey, save it for when you really need it.

CHESTNUT

Oh dear – there's no hiding the fact that this is a miserable wood which burns with a small flame and gives off little heat.

Chestnuts are part of the same family as oak and beech and would make good burning wood were it not for the fact that they can spit like a llama. No problem in a wood-burning stove perhaps, but not on an open fire.

You will find both horse and sweet chestnuts and, strangely, they are not related. The horse chestnut gets its name from the fact that its fruit is similar to that of the sweet chestnut.

Chestnut is not usually cultivated for firewood but coppiced on a twelve-year rotation and the harvest used for fence posts.

At least it is easily worked and split with little difficulty.

Some have made a healing balm for varicose veins and haemorrhoids from horse chestnut by collecting the leaves at the time of a full moon.

The chestnut makes for a remarkable tree to look at, but not to burn.

ELM

Elm should be split soon after felling because of its high moisture content; at felling it has more water content than wood. It needs to dry for a full two years and even then remains a sluggish wood to burn. You will have to put effort into getting it going, after which it will only burn slow and steady. Some have used it as an overnight log for this reason. Be prepared to sweat if you have to split elm – it is tough stuff.

Dutch elm disease brought the lives of many trees to a premature end. Whereas for many years elm was in plentiful supply for burning, it is now becoming more scarce.

It was reputedly the home of the fairies, which is why Kipling warned, 'Ailim [elm] be the lady's tree; burn it not or cursed ye'll be.' It is such a good wood, if you can get some, that burning it seems worth taking the risk. Not as good as oak, though.

FIELD MAPLE

There are many varieties of maple, but of those found in Europe the field maple produces the hardest wood which makes it a good wood for burning, producing plenty of heat and a decent flame.

According to some, maple will strengthen your liver and the branches will keep bats away from your house. It is beloved of wood-turners and carvers, and harps and other instruments are often partly made from it.

HAWTHORN

This is hot stuff, one of the best and hottest firewoods, and for that reason it was often used in 'faggots' (see p 44) or as kindling. It was said to be the finest wood for bringing a wood oven up to temperature. It is a slow burner too, which only adds to its usefulness.

Hawthorn was said to be sacred to the fairy folk. The blossom was supposedly erotic, but its associations with witchcraft gave it a reputation for being unlucky.

HAZEL

There is plenty of magic to be found in hazel wood, and a good deal of heat. It burns fast and generously when well seasoned. For the forester it is a useful wood because it responds well to coppicing, and by regular cutting the life of the tree can be prolonged over many generations.

Be aware, though, that you are dealing here with the 'Tree of Immortal Wisdom' and that all kinds of tricks can be performed with it, not least the encouragement of marriage and fertility. A forked hazel twig is best known for its ability to detect underground water in the hands of a diviner. It is used for walking sticks and shepherds' crooks, and when young can be woven into baskets. All this makes a traditional stand of hazel a useful and versatile asset. By the way, should you ever require protection from evil spirits,

The hornbeam can grow into the stateliest of trees, or try to tie itself in knots.

then you need do no more than draw a circle round yourself with a hazel stick.

Hazel is one of the first to present its leaves in the spring, and amongst the last to lose them in the autumn.

HORNBEAM

A magnificent and stately tree which burns slowly but gives plenty heat, rather like beech. A good all-rounder, it serves well for making firewood as well as charcoal. It coppices easily and can be cut on a ten- or fifteen-year cycle.

Its timber is pale, almost creamy, and is a hard, strong wood, good for furniture. Because of its strength it was used to make the wooden cogs in traditional water and windmills, and is a favourite with butchers whose chopping blocks are often made of hornbeam.

The oak – instantly recognised, widely loved, giving a long, slow burn.

LARCH

Unusually for a conifer, the larch loses its leaves in the autumn. Unlike other conifers, such as pine, it is only a reasonable burner and certainly needs to be well seasoned. Nor is it very long-lasting, so it is not the best choice for a tick-over fire or overnight burning.

Burning it when not properly seasoned can cause any remaining sap to clog chimneys and flues with a sticky, runny deposit – a potential hazard. At least the smoke wards off evil spirits.

OAK

The might oak, symbol of strength and endurance, seems to be in plentiful supply and is a popular wood for burning. However, it is not the very best. Romantics will speak of a 'roaring oak fire', but the truth is that oak very rarely roars and tends to burn long and

slow with a small flame. That said, it produces a lovely, if not lively, fire and is much sought after. One of its talents is to give off heat even when it is reduced to embers, when other woods would have given up. There is no point burning it green; three years is not too long to let it stand.

Burn the leaves, if you have them, for they are said to purify the atmosphere.

PINE

This is a fast-growing wood and widely found in plantations, often in upland areas. Both pine and deal are used widely in the building trade and large bags of offcuts can be bought quite cheaply – although under no circumstances should you burn building timber which has been pressure treated with toxic chemicals.

Pine can make very good kindling if chopped into smaller pieces. It burns fast and gives good heat, but not for long and a pine log soon disappears. It also carries a reputation for leaving heavy tar deposits in chimneys, creating a fire hazard. Fans of pine will tell you that this is a result of under-seasoning, or not burning hot enough. Remember, in Scandinavian countries, Switzerland and Austria pine is often the only wood burnt through long, cold winters, and chimney fires are rare because they take great care to stack and dry their wood and burn it fiercely.

The smell of pine smoke is evocative and gives pine the title 'the sweetest of woods'. The needles are a source of vitamin C and good for chests.

POPLAR

This is called the whispering or shimmering tree, presumably due to its behaviour in a breeze. Sadly it is not much of a burning tree. It burns only in a dull kind of way, giving off lots of smoke. It's called a 'gofer wood' because as soon as you put some on the fire to have to gofer some more.

Although it was prized by makers of shields, it will probably find no place on your hearth, even if it was the wood from which Christ's cross was made; the tree is said to quiverer when it remembers this fact.

SYCAMORE

This is a good burning wood. Sycamore trees were sacred in ancient Egypt, but you'll find plenty of people these days who don't love

them and consider them weeds. However, this is good news for wood-burners as it grows with great ease and there rarely seems to be a shortage of it. It makes a good flame, on a par with ash, but the heat output is not as great.

When young it can often be found in hedges and the prunings can make excellent kindling when seasoned for a couple of months.

WILLOW

Willow grows fast and easily, but it does not burn well and is best avoided, even if well seasoned. Some have described it as 'the worst wood for burning, ever'. It will plop and spark at you. It's not very nice stuff.

Willow grows best and fastest near water and, not surprisingly, when first felled it reveals itself to be a soppy wood requiring lengthy drying.

If you want to make a wish, you should first ask permission from the willow tree by taking a shoot and tying a knot in it while making the wish. Your wish might be to have anything other than willow to burn on your fire. Remember to undo the knot when the wish has been granted.

Having said all this, willow is now finding favour with growers of biomass – a generic term which includes organic matter such a wood and straw used as a heating fuel to warm homes and drive power stations. On a domestic scale biomass is not burnt as logs but as small, dried pellets in specially designed boilers. It is a low-carbon way of producing heat, the theory being that the carbon dioxide given off in the burning process is the same as was absorbed over the years it took to grow. The speed at which willow grows means that biomass can be speedily harvested at three- or four-year intervals.

YEW

Yew gives off a fierce heat and it is a slow burner too. It takes a long time to dry but is a great addition to the woodpile. A large log of yew will last the night. It is not a wood for quickly starting a fire but is a great addition once the fire gets going.

It has long been associated with magic, death and rebirth, and giant yew specimens are often found in churchyards; they may be centuries old. It is described as the hardest of the softwoods. it is good for carving and due to its springiness was often used for bows.

Remember that all parts of this tree are poisonous apart from the berries. Some report illness after inhaling large quantities of yew smoke.

6 | The Axe

THE AXE HAS always been the woodsman's best friend. The chainsaw has, of course, eclipsed it, and few will now make the axe their first tool of choice when a tree has to be felled.

Even so, it is worth holding a modern axe in your hands, weighing it and considering for a moment this direct link with Stone Age man. The axe was amongst the first hand tools ever invented. How and when is anybody's guess, but once discovered it was the tool of choice for over a million years. It had no handle, haft or shaft as your axe does, but it worked in exactly the same way as a modern axe, using a hard edge propelled by human force to inflict a wound on timber, animal, or possibly one another. It was also used to dig, prepare skins for clothing, and for defence as well as ritual. Its versatility has been likened to that of the Swiss Army Knife and wherever the remains of early man have been found, axes have also been discovered. It is our most ancient tool with which we carved our civilisation. If that thought implants a little more respect for the axe in your hands, so much the better. An axe is no crude tool and using it effectively is a skill perfected over millions of years.

As a means of cutting, little has changed in principle in the intervening millennia since that formative day when someone first bashed two stones together and broke one of them into pieces. The first hand axes employed stone, and later flints were chosen to comfortably fit the palm of the hand and with a suitable sharp edge to do the cutting – much tougher than stone. At first man did not work out that the addition of a handle increased the power of the axe by leaps and bounds, and so the handheld axe held sway till nearly 4000 BC when stones with naturally formed holes in them had handles attached. Much spirituality was connected with stones and flints with holes in them, and these so-called 'shaft-hole axes' were more likely to be ceremonial than practical, but it was one more step along the road leading to the axe of today.

The Bronze Age, which ended around AD 500, saw the replacement of stone and flint by copper and bronze, although the shape of the axe didn't change much. A socket was used for attaching a handle in a small but hugely significant step which gave the axe increased strength and power. With the coming of the Iron Age, from around 500 BC in Europe, the axe head developed away from the use of a socket – although early Iron Age axes copied Bronze Age ones – and a hole through the axe head carried the shaft. Any developments since then have been subtleties of shape, strength of metal, and improved methods of sharpening, as well as an understanding that different applications required the axe head to operate in slightly different ways; a battle axe designed for warfare did not serve the job of chopping wood as well as something designed specifically for the task of removing your enemy's head.

Perhaps because of its significance in the development of human life on earth, some cultures hold the axe to be an item of near religious significance. The Ancient Greeks believed that the axe was a thunderbolt sent down from the heavens by the god Zeus, and it's quite easy to see why: a tree that has been split by a bolt of lighting might well look to an Ancient Greek like timber which has been split by an axe. In fact, Greek mythology believed that the true inventor of the axe was Daedalus, who also invented carpentry.

In both the Chinese and Cretan cultures trees were revered and seen as spirits which came and went with the changing of the seasons, which may explain why the axe, which could destroy them, was worshipped. Chinese mythology goes further and credits the birth of world itself with the actions of an axe, swung by the giant Pangu, which spilt an egg in half, the white flying high to create the sky and the heavier yolk sinking to form the earth.

The soldier who guarded Roman magistrates, the lictor, carried a bundle of rods as a symbol of his authority; amongst the rods was an axe, reminding all who disobeyed him of his power to inflict death. These rods, called fasces, can be seen in the symbols of Scandinavian police forces, and the French coat of arms. The word 'fascism' was coined after Mussolini took up the symbol.

Inevitably, given their mythical powers, axes attract superstition:

Don't bring an axe into the house or it will invite death.

Bad luck follows a dream involving an axe.

Protect your livestock by letting them walk over an axe when they first head for fresh grass in the spring.

An axe placed under a sick bed will cure a fever.

Black rain clouds can be punctured by waving an axe at them.

It is bad luck to step on an axe.

A thrown axe will ward off hailstorms and protect crops.

To cure yellow fever, place water in a bath and stand an axe head in it; then, balance three black horsehairs and a white one on the axe handle.

To ease the pains of childbirth, cross an axe and a hatchet under the bed.

Give an axe to a traveller to wish them luck on their way.

Holding an axe during an eclipse will lead to injury.

An axe suspended from a stake will always point to a guilty person.

If an axe lying on the ground is pointing towards you, it is a sign of misfortune.

Give three hard blows with an axe to a tree stump. If the axe sticks on the third blow, a witch will die within three days.

On Christmas Eve, give three hard blows with an axe to your chopping block and the foxes will leave your chickens alone for the entire year.

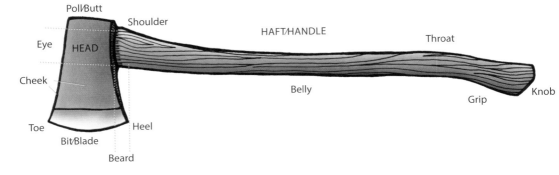

Poll/Butt
Shoulder
HAFT/HANDLE
Throat
Eye
HEAD
Cheek
Belly
Knob
Grip
Toe
Heel
Bit/Blade
Beard

A modern axe.

THE MODERN AXE

There are only two parts to a modern axe: a head and a handle. But there are many combinations of the two and variations in both which can completely alter the working characteristics of an axe. This provided scope for fierce argument at an international gathering of woodsmen. Those attending were asked the question, 'What makes a good axe?' The ensuing argument ran well into the night.

Axes are described by the jobs they are intended to do. From the point of view of the wood-burning enthusiast there are only three to consider, for the rest are craftsman's tools, such as the boat-builder's adze, the carpenter's axe, and the carver's axe.

The woodman's axe has three main jobs to do: cutting down trees, which is done with a felling axe; taking large pieces of wood and reducing them to a size for burning, for which you use a splitting axe; and making kindling, which is best done with a small hatchet, a lightweight version of the axe.

Even within felling and chopping axes you will find huge variations in the shape of the head. The US Department of Agriculture lists no less than thirty shapes of felling axe found across the USA. But for most woodchoppers, the differences are subtle and many axe shapes survive by tradition rather than excellence. Ask a woodsman why he prefers one head shape to another and he will tell that he just does and probably doesn't know why. An axe you know will always seem better than one that is new to you.

A felling axe will have a handle between 28 and 36in with a head weighing 2½ to 3½lbs, making it a middleweight sort of axe. It will have a thin blade will have a gentle taper (called a bevel), so that when felling a tree, for example, the blade can cut deeply and quickly. A properly swung axe will always strike the wood fibres at an angle, never perpendicularly, and so the action of the axe head must not only cut into the wood but get rid of spoil at the same time in order to leave a clean wound for the next cut. There is a balance to be achieved in all axes between the sharpness of the blade and its bevel. A razor-sharp blade with no bevel will simply stick in the wood, whereas a blade with a chunky bevel but a blunt edge will bounce off the tree in disgust.

Splitting axes can come in several sizes ranging, from a 2lb head up to 5lb. The heavier splitting axes are called 'mauls' and the heads can weigh as much as 8lb. The heads are ground to a concave shape so that the blade quickly enters the wood, which then splits apart as the blade thickens.

The hatchet is a much smaller affair, with a 13in handle and a head weighing just 1lb, and is easily carried.

It is also worth mentioning the splitting wedge, which, although not an axe, is a useful addition to the wood-burner's armoury. Using a wedge and a sledgehammer you can at least attempt to split nasty, knotted lumps of wood, which a chopping axe will not touch.

As a general rule, you need an axe with a fairly thick blade if you intend to cut hardwoods, and a thinner one for softwoods. If chopping dry wood your axe might need no bevel at all.

THE AXE HEAD MAKER

If you are purchasing an axe for the first time, and are fully appreciating what a serious business choosing an axe can be, you will be drawn to the mouthwatering options offered by the big Swedish axe makers Gränsfors Bruk, Wetterlings, or Hults Bruk (there are others). Or perhaps the German Helko, or Ochsenkopf,

Germany's oldest axe maker. The choice will be wide. Gränsfors Bruk alone offers axes of various sizes, splitting mauls of varying weights, hatchets for carving as well as splitting, and even axes for throwing; axe throwing is a sport similar to darts in which double-sided axes are flung through the air at targets resembling those used in archery. Then there will be the cheap axes that can be bought in hardware stores and farm equipment shops. Most likely these will be made in China and, while some are built to a standard, it can be difficult to tell the good from the bad.

If you are serious about swinging an axe, buy a good one. Even the best axe costs less than a chainsaw and will repay you handsomely over many years.

But where to go to buy a British-made axe? You won't find one on the shelf, nor on a website. It's not that we have no history of axe making, for they were surely a stock in trade for the metal forgers and tool makers in places where steel once ruled, like Sheffield and the so-called metal-bashing towns of the Midlands. But no longer. Today we look either to forested districts such as Scandinavia or Bavaria if we want an axe worthy of its name.

Josh Burrell
– self taught
master axe
maker.

THE AXE HEAD MAKER: JOSH BURRELL

If you are lucky – and there's a six-week waiting list – then Josh
Burrell will forge you an axe head, and it will be a damned good
one too. This young man, now in his mid 20s, is one of only a
small handful of craftsman who have the skills to take a chunk of
shapeless steel and work the blacksmiths' magic on it to give you
an axe head that is not of only graceful beauty but is a devilishly
lovely tool to work with.

He operates with his father, Graham, from a small forge on the
outskirts of Loughborough. There is no mistaking them as father
and son, as both have identical, bushy Viking-like beards – a
rather dangerous thing to have, you would have thought, when

Axes for all kinds of work – the woodman's best friend.

working all day over a coke-fired forge which spits hot cinders as the temperature of the coal rises. The workshop is littered with iron railings – they are skilled wrought-iron workers too – and massive vintage machines such as the mighty power hammer, which is almost 100 years old and which they have restored to its full working glory. The noise it makes as it smashes into a piece of red-hot steel is deafening and the vibrations must be felt for miles around. It is the sort of kit that would make the earth move for anybody. The atmosphere of this place is one where tradition and craftsmanship come first, possibly at the expense of profit. How can one man and his anvil compete with those super-efficient Swedes who can turn out an axe head in minutes while Josh might labour for three hours? His output is twenty to thirty axes a week.

'I don't remember not being in a workshop,' he explains. 'I know it's dangerous, but I was into workshops ever since I was knee-high to an anvil, always begging my dad to let me come down.'

If you believe that things 'run in the blood', you'll be interested to note that not only is his dad a blacksmith but his mother was a

PLAYING WITH FIRE

goldsmith, his Cornish grandfather was a boatbuilder, an uncle was a potter and another uncle worked alongside the sculptor Barbara Hepworth in her St Ives studio. It all adds up to a rich mix of art and craftsmanship that eventually led Josh to the anvil. Incidentally, Josh tells me that his 4-year-old daughter enjoys nothing better than viewing Power Hammer videos on the internet; so it appears the metalworking gene might already have moved on a generation.

'I briefly went to art college, but it was all conceptual stuff and I had a background of making stuff. I like everything I do to be dictated by a purpose. That's why I fell into tool making. But at art college they told us we couldn't talk about anything that was pre 1980.' He shrugs.

This was too restrictive for a man of traditional talents, so a travelling scholarship from the Prince's Foundation for Building Community gave him experience working alongside craftsmen of all sorts, doing restoration work alongside stonemasons and others.

'I saved up all my money and bought my first power hammer!' He laughs. 'I've got bad shoulders, you see. All aches and pains. It's from being over keen when I was younger, using a hammer that was too big.

'I like forging best, and that's why I like toolmaking because forging is what it's all about. You're supposed to call it "hot work displacement technology" but I call it forging, and it's hard work but you can make a decent living.

'It's an interesting medium, iron and steel, because it's the only craft where you can't touch it while you're working, except glass. But it's interesting stuff with a life of its own, and working it is everything to do with knowing how to apply pressure to it. Wrought iron has got grain, you know, and most people don't think of metal as having grain, but it does. Plasticine behaves exactly like soft metal. Exactly! If I'm teaching others I'll often demonstrate with plasticine.

'I like making tools because they've got longevity. If I make an axe head, I'd expect that to be in use in 200 years time. So I make axes, broadaxes, side axes and carving axes, and heavy-use chisels, that sort of thing.'

A Burrell axe, which proudly carries Josh's stamp, is not made merely from a lump of mild steel, as a cheaper, mass-produced axe might be.

'I'll make the body from mild steel, but I'll forge weld onto that a piece of medium carbon steel. It's much harder than mild steel and it will keep its edge better.'

We moved from his paper-strewn dusty office, where we had been talking over mugs of tea, out into the workshop. His first job was to use one of his own axes to split fine pieces of kindling to light the forge. Once blazing, he added charcoal and applied a draught from an electric fan. The charcoal started to crackle and once the coke was added to the fire it soon became a dull red, yellowing as the temperature rose. The block of steel started at a precise 50 x 30 x 150cm long. It was impossible to imagine how at this stage a lump of metal so ordinary could turn into something as extraordinary as an axe.

The red-hot metal was grasped in tongs and taken across to one of the much-loved power hammers, where the hole which would eventually take the handle was driven through. Then it went back in the fire till it was red-hot once more, and then to the anvil where Dad grasped the sledgehammer and brought it down repeatedly on the tool. The shape of an axe head slowly started to emerge. Then back into the heat it went, then back to the power hammer, Josh skilfully shifting the hot metal so that each blow of the hammer fell onto a different part of the emerging blade creating a familiar outline.

Then came the forge welding, which brought the two kinds of steel together to give the blade a more durable edge. This was teamwork with both father and son grafting as one to make a weld that nothing could possibly pull apart. 'I like being the striker,' admits Graham, performing as the sledgehammer man. 'I'd never done it until Josh started making tools, but I quite like it.'

'A good axe has to have edge geometry,' Josh explains. 'It can be sharp, but useless if the geometry isn't right.'

This is why Josh's moving of the hot metal under the hammer is far more subtle that it might appear, for every resounding stroke is moving the metal in one direction or the other, a fraction of an inch at a time, hopefully in the direction of that perfect shape that Josh craves.

'They always used to send out axes blunt and expected the professionals who used them to know how to put an edge on them. But these days they don't have the skills or they haven't got the kit, so I sharpen mine before they go off.' He rolls back his sleeve. 'Look, no hairs. That's because I test every axe on my arm before it goes off.

'If you're doing a heritage craft like this, its got to have some spirit behind it. The things have got to be made to a higher quality. You've got to pay attention to the balance and the finish.'

After three hours the axe head is done and his last job is to make his mark on it.

'Making tools is a serious business, and there's no leeway. It's either right or wrong. It either works or it doesn't. There are no two ways.'

Brian Alcock – master grinder after a lifetime grinding blades from scalpels to axes.

THE AXE GRINDER: BRIAN ALCOCK

Having 'an axe to grind' generally means having a strong personal opinion. Well, master axe-grinder Brian Alcock, now in his seventies, has got pretty strong opinions on the way blades are sharpened these days.

There was a time when Sheffield, once the city of steel, was full of blokes like Brian. There was also a time when dark, gloomy, sooty, smelling-of-hot-metal workshops like his could be found littered across this city. The cutlery trade back then was a job for individuals, self-employed people, and not the mass production business it has become. Blades were ground by hand, polished by hand, and the handles fitted by hand. Men and women worked long hours in small spaces, buffing (polishing) spoons, shaping forks, and turning out the best cutlery in the world. Brian Alcock started in the trade fifty years ago and never left it. The fact that most of trade has left him behind makes him a rather lonely figure, for there's little place for craftsmen like him in mass production.

Dominating his workshop is his massive grinding stone, nearly 6ft in diameter when new and bought twice a year from Eastern Europe. It is powered by a thundering electric motor, which dims the lights all around when it starts up. At the back end of the machine is a seat which Brian straddles as if he were riding a horse. Inches away from his legs the grinding wheel spins, powerful enough to remove flesh as far as the bone in seconds with little effort. This is not a job for careless fingers.

The scene cannot have changed much in a hundred years. The workshop he is in sits on one side of a courtyard with small units on all sides. These would once have housed countless artisans, skilled in the cutlery trade. They are now studios for photographers, artists and web developers – the self-employed craftsmen of the twenty-first century.

The way Brian sharpens tools is how all blades, not only axes, were once ground. 'I've done t' lot,' says Brian. 'Cutlery, gutting knives for t' fish trade, butchers' knives. In fact I reckoned I've just about ground anything that cuts.'

You won't find the words 'little mester' used anywhere else other than in Sheffield. They are a true, rare breed and Brian may be the last of line. The 'mesters' were specialised craftsmen, the backbone of the industry, who worked for themselves and sold their special skills to the cutlery makers. They rented their own space, created their own workshops, and the best of them were held in high regard. This method of working suited the cutlery industry since when orders were thin factory owners were not paying wages to staff who had little to do. For its time it was a forward-looking way of working. Doubtless many of his modern artisans neighbours are

A grinder's hand applies subtle pressure to achieve a perfect cutting edge for an axe.

employed in pretty much the same way that Brian has worked all his life – on a piecemeal basis.

The little mesters were the middlemen in the production of all kinds of blades. In the case of cutlery it would be the forger who fashioned the blade, the grinder who put the edge on it, and the cutler finished the blade (employing armies of 'buffer girls' to give them a shine) and then he would fix the handle. Brian did the grinding stage, the middle of the process, and is still a master at it.

'How I grind an axe,' he explains, 'depends on what kind of axe it is. If it's a carving axe then I'll just give it a slight radius and a hollow grind. A felling axe needs to be sharper and slightly convex. If it's a chopping axe then I'll give it a broader edge.'

He has no machinery to hold the axe in position as the grindstone cuts, only his hands, which become wet and smothered in the slime that the wet grindstone creates from the friction between metal and stone. He has done this for so long that he cannot describe what he is doing; it is as instinctive to him as writing with a pen.

Some axe heads, I notice, he rolls on the stone more than others, presumably giving a rounder edge, as on a chopping axe. 'You'd soon pick it up,' he says, although I doubt it. 'You haven't got to be frightened of power,' he explains, seated behind the grindstone, riding it like a cowboy, his fingers inches from the couple of tons of thundering, spinning stone. 'I've made blades for the commandos, yer know. And I even did a special one for a big party Joan Collins was having. I suppose it was t' cut t' cake.

'Number of times I've heard people say "t' steak's tough." I tell 'em it's not t' bloody steak that's tough, it's t' knife that in't been sharpened properly.'

Axe users would do well to remember his verdict.

Robin Wood –
carver and axe
handle maker.

THE AXE HANDLE MAKER: ROBIN WOOD

www.robin-wood.co.uk

Robin Wood presents a slender figure, his wide eyes magnified by his circular wire-rimmed spectacles making him resemble a secretive creature emerging, blinking, into the daylight. I found him in his workshop in the Derbyshire peaks, just where the Pennine Way begins. Walkers trot past, largely oblivious to the craft that is taking place inside his stone-built workshop. There are no power tools in this old stable; the floor is littered with discarded timbers – lumps of wood waiting for their turn to become axe handles. There is a row of narrow, pointed tools – the instruments for woodturning, which is another of his skills.

Robin works wood in many ways including turning bowls and plates using nothing but the power of his own foot to turn his pole lathe – a traditional device with which a piece of wood can be spun, a curved, flexible piece of wood acting as a giant spring to provide momentum to the spinning workpiece. The up and down of the turner's foot translates into a forward and backward spinning of the wood, to which one of Robin's dozens of tools is applied, cutting on the forward spin, resting on the backward. It is a mesmerising process, the rhythmic creak of the spring pole, the swish of the cutting edge. No electricity, no motor. This device is known to have been in use in Viking times and the scene in Robin's workshop could have been observed in many past centuries.

Robin's pole lathe is a tribute to George Lailey, who died in 1958 and was Britain's last professional pole lathe turner, a man generally reckoned to be at the top of his game, selling bowls to Harrods. He once said of his apparent lack of interest in profit, 'Money's only storing up trouble, I think. I like making bowls better than I like making money.' The traditional tools that Robin uses can't be bought off the shelf.

'I learnt to forge, harden and temper steel,' says Robin, 'and when I'd done that I made copies of George's tools and then I learnt how to use them.' The inability to buy ready-made tools presents a considerable handicap to a craftsman. Robin Wood found that when he needed tools to carve wooden spoons, for example, he was unable to source the chisels and gouges: 'I had to go to Sweden!' The irony that he lives a half-hour drive from Sheffield, which only a generation ago was the tool-making capital of the country, is not lost on him.

'A good tool is one that works sweetly. It's difficult to describe but you know it when you use it. You can feel a good tool whistle through wood. Which is closer to my heart, the metal work in making the tools, or the working of the wood? I love both.' He hesitates. 'But I really love the wood, that's where my heart is. I like the idea that it's this thing that grew, and it's an individual. And I think it's important to make something that can be used. Art doesn't do the same thing for me. I'm conscious of the tree and its place in the landscape, where it grew and what's going to happen to it. I'm sort of in between its death and giving it new life.'

Robin Wood –
an axe handle
takes shape.

A finely carved
axe handle
starts from a
rough chunk of
wood.

All of which made me wonder if he felt bad about burning wood, destroying it: 'Not at all. I've always heated with wood, especially when I became aware that it is carbon neutral. And, of course, when I was a forester the wood came free. The best stove I ever had was a wood-fired Rayburn. It was as if it was alive. I used to love the experience of coming home to a freezing cold house and then feeling it slowly warm up. And I liked the whole process of lighting it too. I didn't use matches; I used a sharp flint and a piece of steel to make a spark and used something called "charcloth" to act as kindling. Charcloth I make myself by getting an old bit of cotton, or perhaps jeans, then I put the cloth in a tin, shut it tightly and put it in the fire when it's really hot. The cloth burns, but because there's no oxygen you end up with something a bit like powdery charcoal. I direct the spark from the flint and steel onto that, hope it

The axe handle takes shape, carved with an axe fitted with his own handle.

catches, then give it a gentle blow and watch the fire expand. Dried grass is good for kindling too, and I've soon got a fire. I pick up a flint whenever I'm in an area where there might be one and I'll crack it to see if it's got a good edge because you need that to strike against the steel. It sounds hard work but, honestly, it's as fast as a match. I can have a fire going in less than a minute.'

But my interest was the axe handle, of which Robin is a master carver. He once worked in the famous Hatfield Forest, a remarkable woodland in the shadow of Stansted Airport. It is the only remaining royal hunting forest, used for sport as long ago as the Norman kings. That scholar of rural history, Oliver Rackham, described it as being 'of supreme interest in that all the elements of a medieval forest survive: deer, cattle, coppice woods, pollards, scrub, timber trees, grassland and fen. It is almost certainly unique in England

and possibly in the world.' In this heady and historical atmosphere Robin Wood learnt to understand trees, and thereby wood.

His axe handles start as rounds of timber cut to length directly from trees, and it is almost impossible to imagine how the fine curves of an axe handle can be bestowed on this clumsy lump of timber. He first splits the round of timber by placing his axe on it and, using another roughly hewn bit of timber as a mallet, brings it down on the axe and watches as the timber splits obediently to his will. 'You need fast-grown timber,' he says. 'A nice, straight grain and something a bit springy about it.' His wood of choice is ash, for flexibility.

When he has split the round into quarters of roughly the right size, he will draw the outline of the handle using a finished one as a template. Then, with a small axe made with a bevel only on one side, making it more like a long-handled chisel, he begins his attack, taking at first large slices then gradually reducing the size to get closer to the finished shape. When taking large slices of wood it appears a crude and inaccurate process, but his command of the tool is such that it soon becomes clear that the same axe is capable of precision work.

It seems only a matter of minutes before a shape emerges, and only a few minutes more before he calls it done. You cannot help but pick it up and feel it in your hand. It is simply begging you to do so. It feels warm, and is a snug fit.

'Ergonomically speaking, the shape of an axe handle is a personal thing. It's a matter of taste. It's all down to aesthetics. You can have a straight handle on an axe if you wish, it will work just as well. They'll try and tell you that there's something special about the shape of the handle, but there really isn't. The thing that really matters is length because that gives you power.'

I found that difficult to believe. I reached out for a straight handle and compared it with Robin's sculpted one. The straight one felt dull whereas Robin's had life to it.

I wonder if all woodsmen who learn their trade in the company of trees in the quiet vastness of forests, become philosophers? There is certainly plenty of time for considered thought.

'There's a big disconnect now between production and consumption.' His point being that we happily throw logs on the fire without considering how the wood grew, who tended it, who chopped it and carted it. 'And that disconnect gnaws at people. They're fundamentally uncomfortable with it. That's why spoon carving has become a popular hobby, and why we're going through this home baking craze. People are craving the analogue – analogue in an increasingly digital world.'

Robin's handle-making is as analogue as it gets, with no measurements, no power tools, nothing much more than a good eye and a sharp axe. The axe handle might appear to do no more than provide the connection between the human limb and axe head, but Robin would argue that he's facilitating a far more powerful link than that.

AXE SAFETY

Be mindful of the power of an axe head on the move. If you consider that a single blow can overcome the inner strength of a lump of seasoned oak, then imagine what might it do to a vulnerable body part. The place for the axe head is either in its holster, in the air, or in the wood, and nowhere else.

Wear safety glasses or goggles, and a hard hat if there are overhanging branches around, or the possibility of them falling.

Dress properly before using an axe. Boots with steel toecaps are good, trainers are possibly the worst thing you can wear. Don't wear scarves or anything that might blow in the wind, get tangled, or distract you. Don't have anything hanging round your neck. If the handle of the axe is wet, or for any reason your hands might be greasy, use gloves and choose a pair that offer the most secure grip.

A larger and more powerful axe is no more dangerous than a smaller one. In fact, a small axe can do you far more damage in certain situations. If, for example, you are trying to chop a round of wood you might choose to stand it on block. If you bring a long-handled axe down onto the wood and miss, the head of the axe is likely to embed itself in the block. That's frustrating, but it's safe. On the other hand, if you miss with a short-handled axe then there is nothing to stop the edge from coming directly towards your body. The safest way to use a short-handled axe is to kneel down to use it, reducing the swinging circle, so that should you miss, the axe falls into the block and not onto your leg.

Your axe should have some kind of cover for its head, often called a mask, sheath or holster. They are usually made of leather and should be capable of being fitted quickly and easily. A cover that is tricky to put on will never get used. If you are taking a break for a short while, and the sheath is out of reach, then the axe can be safely parked in the cutting block, ensuring that the full length of the blade is buried. Never bury an axe in the ground. If you don't have a sheath, you could use a split length of piping. Blades rust quickly and an axe should never be left out overnight without protection.

The most dangerous axe is a blunt one. Keep it sharp. Wooden handles can be kept 'fresh' with linseed oil.

Never use an axe if the head is even the slightest bit loose. Also check the handle, looking for splits or cracks. Do that at the start of every day's work.

Stop work if you are feeling tired. You will work more effectively after a rest.

The biggest dangers when chopping wood occur when your swing misses the target, or chunks of wood and splinters go flying. Also, accidentally letting go of an axe can cause damage over a wide radius.

Before chopping, look all around you. Remember that people may walk into your work area and allow for it. Check for overhanging branches or anything that might get in your way. Check you footing to make sure there's no chance of a stumble. As a rule of thumb, make sure there is nothing close to you within three axe lengths, plus the length of your arm.

Never allow anyone to stand directly in front of you while you are chopping.

Use a solid and stable chopping block and make sure it sits evenly on the ground.

Place the wood that you wish to cut towards the edge of the block furthest away from you – then if you miss the axe will land on the block instead of heading towards you.

Have in the back of your mind what might go wrong. The axe could slip out of your hand or bounce off the timber, splinters might fly. Quickly think through what would happen if any of those were to occur and don't trust to luck.

If carrying an axe, don't put it over your shoulder like they do in the movies unless you want to lose your head if you fall. Instead, carry it by your side with the blade uppermost and pointing away from you so that you can let go of it quickly and easily if you trip. If you are walking on a slope, carry the axe on the downhill side and toss it aside if you stumble.

Another way to carry a shorter axe might be to hold the head in your hand, blade pointing forwards, and let the handle of the axe rest in the crook of your elbow.

To pass an axe to another person, get hold of it by the knob end, furthest from the blade, with the head nearest the ground and the blade pointing directly at neither of you. Don't let go till the other person signals that they have a good grip on it.

Never leave an axe lying flat on the ground, or against a tree or a building where the edge is exposed.

Use your axe only for chopping. It is not a hammer, nor it is a wedge.

If working in very low temperatures, the head can become brittle. Warm it up gently with a little light work before attacking anything of a size.

SHARPENING AN AXE

With a brand-new axe, it might be a good idea to quickly make a cardboard template of the bevel so that when you eventually have to restore it you have a pattern to work to. There seems to be as many ways to sharpen an axe as there are to bake a cake. Some owners will only use a file, others won't touch one. Some use emery paper, while others will shun it. Whatever you decide to use in the end, the process is essentially a simple one of getting rid of imperfections in the blade which are causing it to cut badly, and then restoring it to its original sharpness. All these processes involve the removing and reshaping of the steel.

The condition of the axe head will determine the tools you need. If you have a powered grindstone so much the better, but make sure it is a slow revolving one kept cool by immersion in water. The danger of using a powered sharpener is that you can overheat the head and cause it to lose it's temper, which means it becomes soft and will be blunt again the first time you use it. The symptom of overheating is a blueness to the steel. If that occurs, you have a lot of work on your hands to get back to tempered metal. Do not be tempted to use an electric angle grinder, which will guarantee a ruined edge.

You can achieve a decent sharpness on an axe with just a couple of tools – a file and an axe stone or grind stone. To those you can add diamond studded files, if you wish, and grinding paste, to achieve a perfect finish. But for putting a decent edge on an axe during a working day, a file and a stone will do the job. You will need a flat file, called a bastard file (which means a file that is neither coarse nor fine and is a loose term), and a long one is easier to use than a short one. It will usually have a coarse and a fine side although it will be the fine side that you will be using most. Filings can build up during the cutting process and clog the teeth and then you will sense the filing getting sluggish. A wire brush is handy to keep the file clean and cutting well. It might be worth fitting a collar, or guard, where the blade meets the handle for you are going to be filing towards the axe head and should it slip then the blade will be coming towards your fingers, and a collar will stop that. For complete safety you should wear stout gloves. Hold the axe in a vice so you can use both hands, although in a conventional vice the blade will then be pointing upwards making it less easy to file. If you can contrive something that will hold the blade horizontally, filing will be easier.

Always pushing the file away from you, try to restore the original bevel remembering about the precious nature of the temper and always allow time for cooling. Sharpen away from you, cutting on the away stroke and lifting the file from the head when you bring it backwards. Try not to cut repeatedly in the same place, but swing the file the length of the bevel so that you are cutting with a flowing, curving motion. Don't be tempted to file too far up the blade and create too narrow a bevel or you will find your axe sticks when cutting. Also, keep changing sides because if you file one complete side and then the other, you are almost certain to get differing grinds on either side of the axe head. This stage of the process is called cutting back and you should examine the head at frequent intervals to make sure you are getting rid of all the nicks and cracks which were making your axe blunt in the first case. Try and follow the bevel the axe maker first gave to the axe – don't try and guess your own.

You will now need a grinding stone. These usually come in oblong shapes intended for grinding smoothing plane blades. If you can get a round one that you can hold in the palm of your hand then some say it is easier to use, and you can carry it in your pocket ready to put an edge back on your axe if your chopping session is a long one. The advantage of the flatter, oblong stones is that they keep your finger ends further away from the cutting edge. Some stones are lubricated with water, some use oil. Use the coarse side of the stone, rubbing the length of the blade in a circular motion. Once you are getting close to an edge, switch to the finer side of the stone to create a finish.

For the finest edge, of the kind you might need on a carving axe, you can use axe handle-maker Robin Wood's technique. You need three grades of wet and dry paper, 800, 1200 and 2500, which can be bought with an adhesive backing to allow you to stick them to blocks of flat wood or MDF. Start with the 800 grit; lie the axe flat on a block and then stroke the wet and dry paper along the blade to polish the edge. Robin looks for the scratch he is creating and checks now and again to make sure the scratches get as far as the cutting edge. The 800 grit is the one you will spend most time with and you shouldn't change to a finer grit until you are sure you have done all the cutting away that you need. Repeat on the other side of the blade. You are now getting to the stage where you will have to watch your fingers.

With the 1200 grit, remove all the scratches you made with the 800 grit, and finish off with the 2500 grit, at which point the bevel with start to sparkle. For perfection, give it a final finish to get rid of any traces of burr by using metal polish spread on a board and used in the same way as the wet and dry papers.

FITTING A NEW AXE HANDLE

If the old axe handle has broken off in the head, then you first job is to remove all traces of it. Drilling it out is best; burning it out is the worst, for too much heat will spoil the temper of the steel. If glue has been used, get rid of all traces of that too and make sure that the hole in the axe head is bone dry.

If you are lucky, your new handle will fit the hole but it is most likely that you will have to do some carving to make a proper fit. If the handle is too small to start with, discard it – it will eventually become dangerous. Wood swells as it takes up moisture, so a damp handle that makes a perfect fit will soon become a loose one. Wobbly axe heads are sometimes fixed by immersing the head in water to allow the wood to take up. This is a fool's errand for when the wood dries, as it eventually will, it will shrink even further. If you insist on soaking your axe handle, then use linseed oil.

It is important that the line of the handle is the same as the line of the blade and you should check this by sighting down the blade towards the foot of the handle. Once you are sure of this, you can then remove any surplus wood emerging through the axe head, and

> 'GIVE ME SIX HOURS TO CHOP DOWN A TREE AND I WILL SPEND THE FIRST FOUR HOURS SHARPENING THE AXE.'

ABRAHAM LINCOLN

then scribe it across its widest part with a chisel to create a cut into which you can drive a wedge, which can be made of steel but dried oak is traditionally used. If both are used, the iron wedge should be driven diagonally across the head of the handle, and not in the same direction as the wooden wedge. Now drive the wedge home till it will go no further and remove the surplus.

HOW TO LOVE YOUR AXE

A well-made axe with a finely forged head and a crafted shaft should last anyone the best part of a lifetime, but not if left to rust and only given a second thought when it needs to be used. Gleaned from the experience of axe-makers worldwide, here are the rules maintaining your axe as your best friend.

Keep the handle oiled. Some prefer linseed, others olive oil, although there are many wood oils to choose from. The danger of not oiling is that the handle might shrink and then it won't take much for it to become dangerously loose. Check regularly. Remember that boiled linseed oil does not leave a sticky residue.

Don't leave it outdoors, and whether stored inside or out make sure it is in its sheath

Don't use an axe cold if the temperatures are really low. Warm it by a fire if you have one, or warm it gently with light chopping before starting on heavy stuff.

Don't be tempted to use it as a hammer, or ever hit it with a hammer. That's what splitting wedges are for.

Vaseline can be good for preventing an axe going rusty.

Make friends with your axe. Axes make bad enemies.

The chainsaw brought about the greatest increase in productivity in the history of forestry.

7 | The Chainsaw

WHAT ARE THE sounds you most want to hear in the forest? The chattering birds, the rustling leaves, the creak of tree limbs in the breeze? This splendid cocktail of sounds evokes woodland better than a thousand words can. But you will be hard-pressed these days to find a woodland that is at permanent peace. Where once the only sounds made by man were the swish and crunch of the axe against a tree trunk, these days it will be the rasping sound of the chainsaw as it gobbles away at a tree with the enthusiasm of a hot spoon melting ice cream. The old boys who laboured all their lives with cross-cut saws, slicing backwards and forwards for many back-breaking hours on end, could not even dream of the ease with which a modern chainsaw can cut wood.

We acknowledged in the previous chapter that axes make bad enemies; chainsaws are even more dangerous monsters, despite the labour-saving transformation they have brought about in forestry management. No tree can survive their attack, and nor can any human. If a running chainsaw catches your skin, it is reckoned that it removes from your bones one pound of flesh every second. For this reason alone, it is worth putting a lot of effort into ensuring the chainsaw remains your friend and doesn't turn into your enemy.

Handsaws have been found in tombs in ancient Egypt. They were made of copper which would have rendered them hardly effective. But flints and other sharp-edged items like shark teeth might have been used before then. The steel saw did not appear until the seventeenth century, and there is no evidence that handsaws were

Properly dressed for chainsaw work – and properly trained.

used at all in forestry before the sixteenth century. Until then, the axe ruled supreme. However, the handsaw, which worked by both pushing and pulling, was first sketched by Leonardo da Vinci around 1500, but such saws were only employed in the cutting of trunks into planks, and not for felling or trimming trees. Early saws were made by taking a piece of heated steel and flattening it by employing a team of blacksmiths working with several hammers to create a flattened shape into which the teeth were cut. The revolution in saw-making took place in Sheffield in the mid-eighteenth century with the invention of a special type of steel which was hard and springy and on which the teeth could keep an edge. By the 1820s half the saws made in the UK were made in Sheffield, which became the centre of the tool-making industry.

A little earlier, towards the end of the eighteenth century, a device was invented independently by two Scottish doctors, John Aitken and James Jeffrey, called a chain osteotome. It appears in 1785 in John Aitken's *Principles of Midwifery, or Puerperal Medicine*. It had cutting teeth attached to a chain, which was moved by turning a wheel around a guiding blade, much in the same way a modern chainsaw operates. It was a surgical instrument used for cutting bone. It was further developed by a German, Bernhard Heine, who had the idea of making the chain into a loop, thus taking a major step towards the modern chainsaw. It remained, however, a tool of the operating theatre, and forestry had over half a century to go before it recognised its value.

The modern chainsaw had to wait until 1926 when another German, Andrea Stihl, patented a two-person saw powered by electricity. But the chainsaw was not an overnight success. The early models were very heavy and needed a man on each end, and the engine proved highly unreliable. At 60kg they did not find any favour amongst foresters.

It was not until the 1950s that the first one-man chainsaws were developed, rapidly reducing in weight from 12kg to 6kg as they developed. Once that breakthrough had been achieved, the march of the chainsaw through the forests of the world was unstoppable.

If you are going to cut wood on a regular basis you will need a chainsaw. If the logs come ready cut from your supplier to the size of your stove, you are lucky. But if you are growing your own wood, or have been offered wood for free providing you collect it, a chainsaw is a vital tool.

And this is where I retreat, because the things scare me to death. I hate the noise, I hate the smell, I hate the danger, but I love not having to cut wood with a saw. Reconcile all these things by taking a safety course before you so much as pull the starting cord. You will be told over and over again that providing you understand the saw and its dangers, then they are perfectly safe. It is only when you cut corners and take risks that you are putting your very life in danger.

All agricultural colleges will have a chainsaw course that will teach you operation and servicing.

8 | Cutting, Chopping and Stacking

HOW TO SWING AN AXE

THIS IS WHERE the hard work begins and there is much scope to do damage to yourself and those around you the moment you raise an axe into the air. Take note of the warnings, which are widely accepted and based on many generations of bitter and painful experience.

First make sure that the area around you is clear; this is important at all times but especially if you are new to swinging an axe when there is a greater possibility of random blows being struck, and possibly axes going flying. Remember also to look not just around you but also above, and beneath you for holes into which you might stumble. A good footing is essential.

How you hold the axe will depend on whether you are left- or right-handed, but one hand grasps the handle just above the knob with your palm upwards so it is facing you. Next, get hold of the axe with your other hand, grasping it a short distance below the axe head, this time with your hand facing away from you. This is the starting position. Try to relax. You need a firm grip but if your hands are too tight or tense then the subsequent movements are either not going to work or will expend far more effort than necessary. Chopping wood is hard work and you must take every opportunity to make it easier on yourself.

Once you have the axe gripped, you raise it above your shoulder, not your head. Which shoulder will be determined by whether you are right- or left-handed – one will feel comfortable and the other

The starting position – hands well apart.

Bring upper hand down towards the lower hand as the axe starts to fall.

Both hands at the bottom end of the shaft as the axe strikes the wood. Note the position of the feet – if he misses the axe will not bury itself in his legs.

won't. Some professional axe swingers learn to work one particular way; others frown on this, believing all axe work can be done either right- or left-handed.

You should keep your eye on the spot you are aiming for. Your aim, and the ability to repeat it, is every bit as important as the power you give to the swing. If you are removing limbs from a felled tree, for example, you need repeated cuts in the same place every time if you are ever to part the branch from the tree. Misdirected blows are a waste of effort.

With the axe over your shoulder you are now ready to make the swing. Bring the axe down and as you do so you will find the hand nearest the head wants to naturally work its way down the handle as the axe travels. Let it do so. By the time the axe head hits the wood, your hands will have met close to the knob. This method provides the least shock to your hands, wrists and arms – important if you are chopping all day long – and provides the greatest momentum to the axe head.

This technique is used for splitting and chopping wood, but if you have a lying branch, or trunk, then you need to master both the forehand swing and the backhand swing, and this may take some time.

The forehand swing cuts the right side of the notch and, for right-handers, starts with the axe over the right shoulder. The cut is taken as described above. In order to cut the left-hand side of the notch, you need to employ the backhand swing. Again, raise the axe over your right shoulder but lean your body to the left and this will bring the axe down onto the left-hand side of the notch you are trying to cut.

It is tempting to think only of the force you are applying to the wood, but this can be the least part of successful axe work. Accuracy is crucial in being able to make repeated blows in exactly the right plac, and it is important to approach the task in a relaxed way, using a natural rhythm, and then you can keep swinging all day. There's no harm in giving a good grunt when the axe hits the wood – it gets the tension out of your system.

You will also by now have learnt the truth of Henry Thoreau when he famously said, 'Wood warms you twice ... once when you cut it and again when you burn it.'

FELLING A TREE WITH AN AXE

A tree of considerable size requires a professional to fell it whether using an axe or chainsaw. A falling tree moves with considerable speed, and so does the butt end where the cut has been made. If you get in its way you can be certain you will be the loser. Big trees cannot only fall quickly, but also roll when they hit the ground. This can be unpredictable. Felling a tree in such a way that it drops exactly where you want it is a great skill learnt over many years and you should not attempt to fell a large tree if you do not have experienced help to hand. Professionals use advanced techniques as well as equipment such as ropes to ensure a safe and predictable drop. Do not try to fell a tree of any size yourself.

Having said that, a small tree, up to a foot in diameter and not too tall, or one where the diameter is less than the width of your axe, can provide good practice if the following precautions are taken. Also, check that you have the right to remove the tree. Some trees are protected. Be aware of the law.

Make sure there are no people within a distance of twice the height of the tree.

Are there any power or telephone lines?

Could someone innocently wander into the felling area?

Look for signs that the tree might be rotten in places as this will affect how it falls.

Is the tree lop-sided with more growth on one side than the other?

Take a good look at the tree and the way it stands before even getting the axe out of its sheath. Does it lean already and might that help you? Is there a breeze which might send it in a direction you don't want it to go?

Consider what are called 'widow-makers'. These are dead limbs or branches which might break loose while you are chopping, or they might be the dead parts of neighbouring trees which will be knocked down as your tree falls.

The first cut taken – the tree will fall in this direction.

The wedge of wood being removed is known as 'the gob' and is the hinge over which the tree will fold.

HOW TO CUT

The object is to create a hinge over which the tree can fold, and to do this you cut two notches on opposite sides of the tree, one a couple of inches above the other with the intention that the tree will fold in the direction of the lower notch. Plan for the first notch to be low down so as not to leave lengthy stumps, and not to waste wood. The lower the notch, the less chance of you missing the swing and injuring yourself.

Make the first cut downwards at 45 degrees, then cut again around the tree and along the same line till you are halfway round.

Working from the other side, a similar cut is made above the line of the gob.

'Timber!'

Then cut round again but this time a couple of inches higher with the intention of getting the axe deeper into the wood.

Then cut around again another couple of inches higher, all the time making the cut deeper.

You then need to clear the notch, also known as 'the gob', but don't try to cut upwards, which is dangerous, but cut more perpendicularly to the tree till the spoil has been cut free. You should now be no further than halfway through the trunk. The secret is not to take wild swings but accurate ones.

When you are satisfied with the first notch, go round the other side of the tree and make the second notch, ensuring it is a good 2in higher at its base than the first. Cut it in the same way, taking a little of the wood at a time, working round the tree, then again a little further up the trunk. As you approach halfway, pay attention in case the tree should suddenly fall. Once the upper notch is halfway through the trunk, it is quite possible that the tree will collapse under its own weight. If not, you can probably push it over. Be sure never to stand directly behind a falling tree as the movement of the butt end can be unpredictable.

Once the tree is safely on the ground, the next stage is the removal of the branches, in a process known as limbing. This can be dangerous since you are going to have to remove the limbs with glancing blows rather than direct hits, and there is potential for the axe to slide. Don't stand astride a log, but work from one side and keep the log between you and the axe. Fallen limbs can be under compression or tension, depending on the way the tree has fallen, and once you start to cut they can move unpredictably. In order to get clear access to the log, you might want to remove the small branches first which you should do by cutting in the direction in which the branch lays. Start at the bottom end of the tree and work upwards.

Once you have cleared the branches of your log, it is perfectly possible to chop your log into smaller rounds which you will then split into firewood. But it is an advanced technique which requires you to stand on the log and chop between your feet. For this reason, you should only try this when you think you have complete mastery of the axe. Most modern woodsmen will use a chainsaw for this.

SPLITTING WOOD

This is often called 'chopping' wood, but chopping is when you cut across the grain as in 'chopping down a tree'. If you are cutting in the direction of the grain, as in firewood production, then you are splitting.

For this you will use splitting axe rather than a felling axe, and if the rounds are of a substantial size then wedges and a sledgehammer will be needed too. Don't be tempted to use your axe as a wedge and start hammering down on the head, for nothing is more certain to destroy a good axe. All the safety suggestions for felling trees apply for splitting too.

Choose a good piece of heavy timber for your chopping block. In fact, two blocks can be useful; the second acts as something against which you can lean your axe or sledgehammer when not using it. You are going to be doing enough bending and lifting, and don't need to create any more.

A chopping block is essential and you should invest time in finding a suitable piece of wood of the right size for you. If you try to split wood that's standing on the ground, part of the energy is dissipated in driving the wood a little way into the ground and that is energy wasted. Your block should be considerably wider than the wood you are trying to split. The variety does not matter but hardwood will be better. It should stand no higher than your knee and the object is for the axe head to be horizontal as it strikes the wood. It can be helpful if the top of the block is not cut entirely square. Most rounds of timber will tend to lean one way or the other when you stand them upright, so having a slight slant in one direction or the other gives you the opportunity to place the round in the most stable position before splitting.

Stand the wood you want to chop on the far side of the block then, if you miss, the axe will hit the chopping block and not you. Examine the wood carefully, and look for existing cracks for these will be the places where the wood will part mostly easily. This is where you should aim your first blows. Don't aim for the centre of the wood, aim for the edge furthest away from you if the round has any width. Try to give the axe a little twist just as it hits the wood; this needs practice but if done properly a little of the axe's momentum goes into forcing the wood apart and at the same time prevents the axe from sticking in the wood. Once you have your round of wood in two pieces, it is almost certain you will want to split each of them again. If you can safely stand them on their end, you can chop them in the same way as before but it might be easier to lie one piece across the other and, being careful to attack it from the far side, then split it lengthways remembering to give the axe the twist that parts the wood.

If you are cutting a wide round of timber, it is unlikely that your first blow will split it in two, but if you have created a weakness along the grain then that's good enough. Make that first blow on the far side of the wood, then try and make the second blow on the side of the wood nearer to you so that the first wound is in line with the second. This way you have weakened the wood all the way across and with luck the next blow will divide it. For a round of a huge diameter, splitting across the middle may be impossible. Wood like this is best chopped from the outside towards the middle, one chunk at a time.

MAKING IT EASIER

As if the swinging of the axe didn't require enough effort, you will also find yourself doing a lot of bending and lifting to place the split wood back on the block for further splitting. This can be equally hard work and if you are beginning to tire it can be the last straw. Try this old trick and save yourself some sweat. Make sure your chopping block is wide enough to carry an old car tyre and place this on the block. It might be useful to have some way of attaching it to the block, perhaps with coach screws, so you don't have to repeatedly pick the tyre up as well. Choose the tyre to match the size of the rounds you are cutting. Now chop your wood and see how the tyre holds it in position so that you can make repeated blows without having to reposition the round. This way you can reduce a whole round of wood into pieces of the right size for your stove without once having to bend down.

Another way to achieve the same result is to make yourself an elastic belt out of a stout piece of rubber attached to a length of chain. The other end of the rubber strip has a hook attached. Place the rubber round the timber and drop to hook into on of the chain links to hold it securely. You can now chop away and all the pieces will stay in one place allowing you to reduce an entire round to firewood without once having to handle the wood.

WHEN THE AXE GETS STUCK

This is most likely to happen if you try to split a particularly knotty lump of wood, which all trees deliver sooner of later. If you are lucky you will be able to free it with a gentle twist to and fro, being careful not the weaken the handle. Somewhat gentler on the axe is to use the palm of your hand and bring it down sharply on the knob end of the axe handle.

USING WEDGES

If the round is proving to be particularly tough and several blows with the axe have failed to split it, then you may have to resort to wedges, which should be part of the woodsman's kit. It might be tempting to use the axe to drive the wedge into the wood but this is an almost certain way of ruining the axe. Instead, use a piece of timber roughly shaped like a hatchet – any hardwood will be plenty strong enough. If that doesn't work, then resort to a properly made sledgehammer. If splitting a lengthy log, rather than a round of wood, a couple of wedges driven in along the length of the log might be needed.

FORGET THE AXE

You can buy hydraulic splitters for domestic use which can be powered by hand or run with a small motor. There are also many forms of compressive splitters that require you to wind them up to achieve splitting – these can be effective but slow.

Then there's the halfway house which lies somewhere between the ancient axe and modern hydraulics. If your joints are beginning to ache, or you simply don't feel safe flinging an axe head around, then two inventions might come to your rescue. You should be aware, though, that serious guys who see themselves as the greatest lumberjack the world has ever seen, and as capable of swinging an axe as a valiant Viking, will pour scorn all over you. But what will that matter when you are able to retire to your wood fire of an evening having done your muscles no damage at all?

The Logmatic:
A gentle strike
embeds the
head in the log.

A couple of
strikes and the
log will split.

That's not strictly true, of course, because some effort is required to make both these devices work, although far less than swinging an axe. My guess is that a reasonably fit man or woman would be able to split wood with either of these machines long after they would have put the axe back in the shed and gone for a lie down.

The Logmatic is a single-handed device consisting, essentially, of two stout steel tubes, one of which runs inside the other. Attached to the end of one is the cutting head and this you position to rest on the piece of wood you want to cut. Opinion divides on the effectiveness of these two devices, although the videos you can find on YouTube are persuasive. It is a case of try before you buy, and don't expect you are now empowered to cut the toughest, knottiest lumps of wood. However, I was intrigued and paid a visit to one of its greatest enthusiasts.

Crispin Rogers with his Logmatic and armoury of axes.

THE LOG SPLITTER: CRISPIN ROGERS

www.logmatic.co.uk

Crispin Rogers lives in the chalk uplands of the Chilterns on 4½ acres of his own heavily wooded garden, with access to the local common which provides even more of his timber needs. In every corner of his garden is a stack of wood either drying or waiting for cutting.

Seeking a better and less strenuous method of cutting his sawn logs, he came across the Logmatic, which appeared in a German mail order catalogue. Intrigued, he bought one, loved it, and is now the UK importer of this device, which was invented, and is now made, in Estonia. He is also the Logmatic's greatest advocate. Not only that, he is something of a collector of wood-handling devices. In his garage you will find hydraulic splitters, and giant grippers for holding and rolling logs, and he demonstrates them with great pride. Here is a man at home with handling wood.

He demonstrates the Logmatic by placing a round of wood on a firm chopping block - this needs to have little give in it otherwise the energy of the Logmatic will be absorbed and wasted. He then places the tip of the Logmatic, which is shaped in a broad V like a maul or a splitting axe should be, and then, holding it in place with one hand he raises the outer sleeve and brings it down heavily in order to give the cutting edge a start.

'The problem with using a chopping axe,' he says, 'is that you have to keep hitting in the same place every time. With this, once you've made your mark the blade will sit in exactly the same place for every blow. Also, it holds the log in place. When you chop with an axe the wood can go all over the place.' He then proves his point. Having made his first mark with a lightish thrust, he employs both hands to raise the outer sleeve much higher, then bringing it down with greater force to achieve the split. 'No one has yet been injured with this device,' he says, 'but if you're not an expert with an axe it can go all over the place. Finland has 2,000 axe accidents a year. Most people who buy this are very happy with it.' And he clearly is as he chops away, quickly splitting his logs with little danger to himself or anyone else. And it will not only split logs, but kindling too.

The Logmatic is the new kid on the chopping block.

A small domestic log store.

STACKING WOOD

Is it an art or a science? Either way, it is not only insulting to the wood to store it improperly but it is a huge waste of all the effort put into producing it. If you merely leave it in the open where rain can drench it, eventually you will end up with rot. And even if it doesn't get that far then you have a pile of wood which is never going to catch light and your efforts at making a fire with it will be as productive as setting light to soggy newspaper.

But to go back to the original question, do you need to be a scientist or an artist to get the best result? As you might expect, the answer is that you need to be a bit of both. If you like building houses out of playing cards, or balancing dominoes on top of each other, if you are master of Jenga, which requires precision of eye and steadiness of hand, then you'll probably build a good wood pile. If you know the science of ventilation and airflow, and how a

A good log store should face the sun have a good flow of air and shelter from the rain.

good blast of wind through anything causes dehydration, and if you can add to that a little of the mindfulness of an engineer, then all that science you will also deploy. If you are in the lucky position of being able to bring together all those artistic and scientific talents, you will build woodpiles like the world has never seen.

As far as art is concerned, can any serious wood-burner deny that a good pile of wood is a thing of glorious natural beauty? There is a sculptural element to it; a form created out of odd-sized chunks of timber which, taken apart, appear random, yet when properly brought together have the power to inspire. It is not only with rich colours that a wood pile can glow: it can melt the heart when the low light of an autumn afternoon hits it, or when the setting winter sun casts long shadows between the logs. It speaks to us when the red-breasted robin perches on it. It is saying, 'I am here and I will keep you warm. Fear not the winter for I can draw its sting.'

A woodpile is speaking volumes about you too. You can tell in an instant how much its creator cares about his wood. A psychologist might say a random dump is the product of an idle mind; or a finely judged and balanced pile is the work of someone showing deep respect for his or her fuel. Some go further. In those parts of America where the winters are longer, colder and snowier than ours, you don't look at someone's Facebook page to work out what they're like; you'll give a quick glance at their woodpile. If the pile is square, straight and solid, then that is probably a fair description of the builder. The insecure build their woodpiles low for fear that everything might come tumbling down while the ambitious will build them wide and high. And woe betide anyone who builds their pile so ambitiously high that it topples over, for they will be the local laughing stock for the entire season. It has even been known for a father to go and inspect the woodpile of his daughter's suitor, to see if he measures up.

The Scandinavians, of course, know all this and have for generations. A good woodpile means more there than in most places, for without good wood you will surely starve in the depths of winter. There is no end to their inventiveness. Their heaps can be round like beehives, sometimes with vertical sides and a cone-shaped roof reminding you of old-fashioned corn stacks. Some are merely circular, but all are built with true precision. Employing the differing colours of the ends of the logs, for example, the truly artistic have created piles in the shape of wild creatures, like owls for example. In Switzerland, it is impossible to slither past a chalet without your eye falling on the woodpile built under the overhanging roof to keep the snow off. The wood store is part of the house, as important to family life as the kitchen or larder.

But these wood stores are only for the hugely ambitious – those with large amounts of wood and the labour to create and sculpt. Most of us will have to make do with something simpler, which may come as a relief for building woodpiles is part of the high-latitude dweller's genetics and those of us who live further south haven't quite got it – it doesn't run in our blood like it does in theirs.

A properly
built stack
will be
self-supporting
– this one
needs a roof.

Keeping it simple means that a decent pile can be built in a day and it will last you all winter. You may have one of the many log stores which can be bought off the shelf, and these give good service and require less skill in building your pile.

If you want a freestanding log pile, however, you have to consider the site very carefully. Think of where the sun is during the day and place your woodpile to allow the wood to feel its warmth. There is no point building it in a damp, shady part of the garden as if you're ashamed of it. Unless you have a bricklayer's instinct for the job, choose somewhere where at least something, such as a wall, can give support to one end of the pile, and something to support the back. Imagine children running into it, or a wheelbarrow. Will it survive? Support on at least two sides will help it.

The base is of great importance. Whatever the nature of the ground beneath it, the wood must be raised above it otherwise

PLAYING WITH FIRE

the logs at the bottom will become saturated and rot. The whole point of getting the wood off the ground is to allow air to pass under and up through the stack, drying the wood as it goes. This is the first, and most important principle in wood stacking – keep the air moving through it. You may have some odd-shaped lumps of wood, usually the knotty bits. Rather than regarding them as trouble, you should think of these as your friends. Inserted into the stack they will allow random gaps to form and these in turn will create a better flow of air. Don't stack your wood too tightly. You may be behaving a bit like a bricklayer, but you are not creating an impervious wall: gaps are your friends and will allow your wood to breathe. Also, stack your wood with the bark side upwards, when you can. Think about it: didn't nature put the bark there to keep the rain off the inner wood, and isn't that what you're trying to achieve? However – and here's an argument that could run and run – some say that the bark side should be laid downwards as any moisture trying to evaporate through the wood need to be able to rise. Both are good theories, so you must decide for yourself.

Whatever the shape, the covering is important. A plastic sheet will work, but needs anchoring and will provide a dampening river of rainwater to flow down the ends of the logs. If you can contrive a black-coloured cover, it will absorb just that little bit more of the sun's winter heat, which is always valuable.

Start with some 4 x 2 timber laid flat, or use an old pallet. Straight ash poles would do, but ash makes excellent burning wood and you might want to save that for the fire.

A freestanding pile can to be built like a log cabin, each layer laid at right angles to the last. However, it's not quite that simple because it is easy to create vertical seams which are not tied together in any way and the pile will surely collapse. Instead of criss-crossing all the way along the pile, build two vertical pillars of timber using the log cabin technique, perhaps no more that 5ft high and as deep as you intend the pile to be. Choose the wood carefully using pieces as regular as bricks because the pillar needs to be a strong structure with little wobble. Don't just hope it will be OK because it won't. If the ground is soft enough, you might be able to drive stakes and create your pile between those.

A sheet covering is not ideal, but the old pallets ensure a good flow of air.

Having built four pillars where you want the pile to stand, make sure they feel secure. Then stack your wood between them, taking time over it to make the jigsaw fit together (but not too tightly) and you will have a pile that will stand proud on its own.

A circular pile is attractive and some say it is far easier than building a rectangular stack. Also, for the ground space it occupies a circular stack hold more wood than a conventional one. This design is popular in Europe, particularly in Germany where they are known as *Holz Hausen*, or wood houses. They can be quick to build and the secret lies in the fact that in a circular pile it is only the outside wall which is built and stacked while the inside is merely filled haphazardly with wood. In other words, there's less precise stacking to do.

Start by scribing a circle on the ground of the size you want your pile to be. Do this by hammering a stake at the centre point

PLAYING WITH FIRE

and attach a string to it, then at the distance from the stake where you want to outside of the wall to be, fasten a stick sharpened to sufficient of a point to mark the ground. Then, keeping the string taut, walk round and round till you have a clear groove in the ground to which you can work.

Now you can start to build the wall by placing logs, about a foot long, next to each other, end to end, all the way round till you have a complete circle of logs. Choose regular shaped pieces, as they will be easier to build with and make a more secure wall. The irregular pieces can be used to fill the middle and won't be seen.

To avoid the danger of the wall collapsing outwards, the outside ends of logs, which are creating the wall, need to be a little higher than the inside. You can achieve this by first going round the circle, following its line and laying logs end to end, then building the wall with the outer end of the wall logs resting on the circle of logs you have created. After one revolution, build the next circle on the top of the first and so on, upwards. After two or three rounds you can start to fill the middle by throwing, rather than placing your wood. This makes the circular wood pile one of the quickest to build.

To make sure the walls are vertical, use your eye but remember you are creating a beehive and not something the shape of a tin can. So allow the walls to creep inwards a little by making sure that the wall timbers are always higher at the outer end than the inner.

These circular wood piles are probably the most stable, but can be strengthened even further by inserting a couple of long ash poles, of the same diameter as the stack, and the downward pressure of the wood on them will help prevent the sides from falling outwards.

Once you have reached eye level with your heap, you have probably gone far enough (although the standard German measurement for a *Holz Haus* is 10ft in diameter and 10ft high – this is a lot of wood). Now start to create a domed roof by adding wood to the centre of the heap and then add a layer of plastic sheeting, Then cover this with pieces of wood, bark side up of course, and work these round the circle as if they were roof tiles.

By now you will be master of the construction process. The next giant leap into artistry I will have to leave to your imagination.

9 | The Wood-burning Stove

IT TOOK MANKIND an awfully long time to come up with the wood stove. It is half a million years since hearths were first used to control fire, according to archeologists, and 2,000 years since the Chinese and the Romans discovered that chimneys were a useful way of getting rid of the smoke. Even during the Little Ice Age of 1550 to 1850, the majority of European homes would have been heated with open fires, although the Americans were starting to use cast iron in the early 1700s (the first cast-iron stove was made in Lynn, Massachusetts, in 1642), as were the Germans, but not on a large scale. The breakthrough moment, back to which all modern stoves can be traced, is the Pennsylvania stove of 1744; it really is the predecessor of them all.

It was not the greatest stove ever invented, but it was a game-changer credited to Benjamin Franklin – a true American polymath who combined being a politician, author, thinker, and inventor of both the lighting conductor and bifocal glasses He gave us the first open-fronted stove that really worked, although the Franklin 'Fireplace' might be a more accurate description, although some models were developed with closing doors which gave them a stove-like appearance, and helped with draught control. The design was never patented. He wrote, '… as we enjoy great advantages from the inventions of others, we should be glad of an opportunity to serve others by any invention of ours; and this we should do freely and generously.' Had he been less generous and secured a royalty on every similar fireplace or stove sold since, his fortune would surely

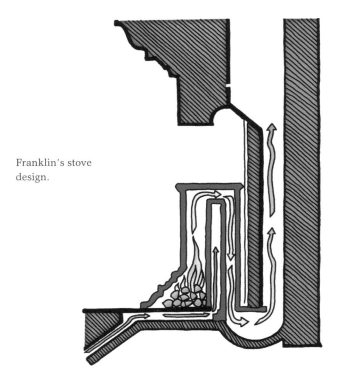

Franklin's stove design.

have made the modern-day techno-oligarchs look poverty-stricken by comparison.

To understand why the Franklin stove was such a huge step forward, it is worth thinking about the workings of the simplest kind of stove, as basic as the early ones would have been. These were no more than a cast-iron box which contained the burning wood with a door through which it could be refuelled, a vent to control the amount of air that entered the fire box, and a chimney to get rid of the smoke. This is about as simple as a wood stove can ever get, and you can make a wood stove out of an oil drum or even an empty gas bottle, as many people have done. But as soon as you start to examine the requirements of a fire that can be controlled, and which gives off the maximum amount of heat, and burns with efficiency, then it starts to get a little more complex.

PLAYING WITH FIRE

Let's think about an oil drum stove with a door, a chimney, and not much else, like the much-loved pot-belly stove – one of the simplest stoves you can find.

There are only two things we can control; the amount of air reaching the fire, and the quantity of wood we choose to burn. To control the air, and in turn the essential oxygen, you need some kind of damper which allows more or less air into the fire chamber. This might be a separate door, or it might consist of holes in the main door some of which can be blanked off as needed. Whichever kind of damper you have, you need to be able to close it fully if you want a fire that is going to be long lasting. As far as the wood is concerned, you can choose larger chunks which will burn less vigorously and for longer, or smaller pieces which can give a hot but short-lived fire.

But there is a little more to the working of a stove than that. As the wood burns, ash will accumulate and this is a good thing. It not only helps to retain heat in the stove, but it keeps a more even temperature throughout the burning chamber. Those who clean out their wood ash every day should remember they are not dealing with a coal fire where an uninterrupted draught is vital. Wood likes to burn on its own ash, so let it build until it starts to limit the space available, and only then clean it out. Firebricks serve a similar purpose, to hold heat within the stove as well as protect the iron from direct flames. A bigger stove, incidentally, is not necessarily a hotter one unless you want to burn uneconomic amounts of wood. If the fire is contained in too large a chamber, it will simply be too far from the stove's walls and much of the heat will be making for the chimney before it has had any warming effect on the metal at all. On the other hand, a small stove requires small pieces of wood which burn quickly, making a small stove a difficult beast in which to build a long-lasting fire. Incidentally, a black stove will radiate more heat than a light-coloured one which explains the wide adoption of dark colours.

The chimney has to be chosen with care, too. Too large and it will rob you of valuable hot air, too small and you will find smoke trying to escape through the door and into your room. Too short and there will be insufficient length to create a proper draught. An uninsulated tall chimney can be a danger, for if that part of the

chimney exposed to cool air is too long, then tar and other sticky substances will condense onto the chimney interior, ready to catch fire if you are unlucky.

Franklin's stove worked on a much more sophisticated principal which he perfected by experimenting with his own fireplace in Pennsylvania. His idea was to lengthen the distance the fire smoke had to travel in order to allow more heat to be transferred from the hot smoke to the air room without any smoke escaping. Anyone who has sat in a cold, draughty house in front of an open fire will know only too well that as the evening progresses so you edge closer and closer to the flames for comfort. This is because the majority of the heat is fast dispersing up the chimney and the rising air is being replaced by a cold draught from under the door. Franklin recognised this and was determined to put all that wasted heat to use.

His idea was to use a baffle, a cast-iron box, around which the hot air from the fire would circulate, capturing heat that would otherwise be lost in the chimney. The baffle itself was hollow and the lower end of it was open to the room air, the upper end having holes through which the warmed air could escape.

Once the fire was going and giving heat, the smoke would rise from the wood (or coal) pass over the top of the baffle before descending to pass down the rear of the baffle, maximising the distance the smoke had to travel. The cool air in the baffle, drawn from the room, quickly warmed. The warm air rose within the baffle and escaped into the room through the vents in the top having been warmed by the hot smoke which would otherwise have gone to waste. To give others their credit, similar stoves using what was called the inverted siphon principle had been exhibited in France and Germany since the mid 1600s.

Although Franklin's stove has the reputation for being a major step forward, this is rather more to do with Franklin's widely respected reputation in other fields than as the inventor of the efficient fireplace. It didn't sell well. The problem was that it was difficult to persuade the smoke to descend down the back of the fireplace unless the fire was burning strongly Once the fire started to go down and the smoke became less hot, it simply wouldn't make the effort to flow round the bend and a smoky room was the result. This was a major problem which Franklin left for others to solve, having established the principle that the heat in smoke must not be allowed to go to waste.

The modern wood stove brings together a little from each of Franklin's ideas. Despite what the persuasive modern manufacturers might tell you, most stoves are still no more than fireboxes with controls to adjust the flow of air. Some will have devised ways of recirculating hot smoke to increase the burning efficiency and the transfer of heat from fire to surrounding air, much as Franklin was trying to do. And that's it. You might find a stove or two on the market which now boasts microprocessors and even remote controls, but what they are trying to achieve are the same ambitions set out by Franklin and the firebox makers who came before him. We have come a long way in terms of efficiency and aesthetics, but not necessarily in principles, and so the advice given here might just as well apply to a fire-maker of a century or more ago.

THE PHILOSOPHY OF STOVES

Keeping a wood stove going is a proper household job, likened by some to having a pet around the house. It needs caring for, and understanding, and while it can be ignored for periods of time it must never be entirely forgotten.

I cannot tell you how to choose a stove, which is a decision akin to choosing a life partner, given that a good stove is capable of giving just as much warmth and affection. You can choose on the basis of looks, and the attractiveness of stoves has advanced in leaps in recent years with the Scandinavians often leading the way. It would be better, though, if you chose a stove to fit your needs, as well as your style requirements. Consider the size of room. Do you want constant or occasional heating? Do you want to link it up to an existing heating system? A good stove dealer will have all this advice at their fingertips, or you can plough through the performance figures if you think your mind can tangle with British thermal units etc. One tip is to work out the size of the room by measuring the length, height and width in metres and multiplying them together to give you the volume. Divide this by fourteen and you will get the rough kW, or kilowatt output, that you need.

Install a simple box burner if you wish, but for serious heating with least waste look for models with features that maximise the transfer of heat from firebox to the surrounding air. 'Airwash technology' creates circulations within the stove which can deflect the flames and smoke away from the glass front, preventing an annoying build up of soot ensuring you always have the sight of a flickering flame to enjoy. Airwash also allows the hot gases to burn to the maximum so no energy is wasted. I have only considered wood-burning stoves in this book, but some stoves offer multi-fuel burning options which allow you to burn coal, coke or even peat.

Running a wood stove is an elemental business. You are dealing with natural products of the wood or forest, then using the oxygen in the air we breathe to turn them into warmth. There is much about wood stoves that is practical, but stoves work at a different and more natural level too, reminding us every time we light them of the small miracle that we are performing and one to which we owe our survival as a species.

There are natural things you must understand and practice. You must know how to make the fresh air your friend, and don't let it be your enemy. Too much air and the wood burns more fiercely and faster than you wish, too little air and in the worst case it will simply go out. It is a very fine judgement that only comes with experience. You need to understand the principles of lighting a stove and keeping it fuelled with just the right amount of wood, and how to keep a fire ticking over during a long, cold night so that it is ready to burst into flame the following morning. The wood itself you have learned to stack and dry till it is almost begging to be burned. You have now arrived at the crescendo of the wood burning operation.

INSTALLING A WOOD STOVE

Unless you are living a frontier lifestyle in a little house on the prairie, your stove will need to be professionally installed. Enthusiastic DIYers have done good jobs and there's no reason you shouldn't if you have the skills and obey the regulations. Check your house insurance is valid if it's a DIY job; some insurance companies will insist a stove in installed by someone with proper certification. Local authorities enforce building regulations which specify in great detail how a stove and chimney should be placed in a house. If you choose to ignore them, and get caught, you face having to pull out the entire installation and starting again. It's not worth it.

There is a lot to consider, not least the chimney which must not only be solid and secure (chimneys are often poorly maintained) and you must take good advice on whether it should be fitted with a steel liner. Although the regulations (in the UK) do not demand it, some installers will insist that your chimney is lined. It can be expensive (which is why some installers can be very persuasive) and might not always be necessary, so satisfy yourself that they are giving you the right advice. Remember that although a liner is a considerable expense, old chimneys can leak both smoke and carbon monoxide, often into upper rooms which the chimney stack passes through. Fixing any leaks will cost far more than installing a chimney liner, apart from the inherent dangers to human life. If it can be shown that the chimney has no leaks (done with proper tests and not of the basis of hearsay) then that might be an argument for not having a liner fitted.

Another argument in favour of a liner is that a conventional open chimney allows the rising air to cool more quickly than a lined chimney would, and this encourages gases to condense and settle on the sides of the chimney producing tar and other flammable compounds, increasing the fire risk. Another problem is that the smoke higher up the chimney, being cooler, can sit there and reduce the upward flow of smoke leading to a poorly burning fire.

If you have any doubts, install a liner and sleep well. If you are lucky you might have a house that was built with a solid, lined chimney and there are no problems with these - they need no liner.

This is not the place to trudge through all the details that the authorities require before an installation meets their requirements, but it is worth noting that a common fault with many installations comes under the heading of 'back wall' problems. A stove must be at least 50mm away from the wall behind it, assuming it is not wood or plasterboard or something else that will catch fire - exactly what is considered to be fireproof will be set out in the regulations. If you have a combustible surface, then 24in is the requirement (these figures may change, so check). Installers can be careless about clearances as it might involve them in extra work to get the stove in exactly the right place.

Regulations also have something to say about the state of the hearth on which the stove sits. If there is no existing hearth (most fireplaces will already have one) then clearly any hearth you install must be of non-combustible material, be broad enough to catch anything that might fall from the stove (the minimum size is 840 x 840mm) and be at least 12mm thick. That applies to a freestanding stove; stoves inset into existing fireplaces have differing requirements which can, at times, appear illogical. For example, there are many stoves, particularly from Scandinavia, which allow you to store logs beneath them. This would appear to be against the regulations if strictly enforced.

If you are installing a wood stove in a house which has no existing chimney, all is not lost. It is perfectly possible to design an exterior chimney which emerges through the outside wall from just above the stove. Planning restrictions may apply and neighbours should be consulted – some, strangely, don't appreciate the scent of wood smoke.

The installation of a wood stove is not done on a blank canvas. You will have to factor into your plans the position of existing chimneys, hearth, floors and walls. If you have to use an existing recessed fireplace, then expect some heat to be lost to the walls, however all is not lost for if you are using your wood stove for long-term heating, the absorbed heat in the walls will remain there for some time, radiating long after the stove has gone out.

GOOD STOVES DESERVE GOOD CHIMNEYS

Best tip for using an existing chimney – get it properly swept before using it for the first time.

We got by without chimneys for countless generations but at great cost to health and life. Back then a hole in the roof to let the smoke escape was all we asked. To a certain extent, it worked even if it was like sitting round a campfire in your own front room. If you want to see the oldest chimney in Britain, then you have to go to Conisbrough Castle in Yorkshire where you will see one dating from ad 1185. They did not become common in houses until the sixteenth and seventeenth centuries and until then people were happy to lightly smoke themselves as they sat round a fire at the end of the day. The harmful effects of smoke inhalation are well known these days, and in parts of Africa where domestic cooking is still done over open fires in confined huts, it is reckoned as a major contributor to early death, particularly amongst women who spend most of their time tending the fire and making food. Before the widespread adoption of chimneys, though, no thought was given to the idea that smoke might not be good for you; in fact, it was seen as useful in keeping birds out of the rafters and might even have a preservative effect on the timber frame of the building.

In England, it was the gentry who first adopted the chimney, around the time of Queen Elizabeth I, and it was considered a courtesy to visiting ladies to provide them accommodation in

a neighbouring house if yours didn't have chimneys and the neighbours did. The ladies' safety, however, was in considerable doubt since the early chimneys were made of wattle and daub, half of that combination being, in effect, kindling. It wasn't until 1719 that it was decreed that all chimneys should be built of brick, although a lining was sometimes needed to prevent the escape of smoke and gases into upper rooms and this was often made of a mixture of lime putty and fresh cow dung.

PLAYING WITH FIRE

The early chimneys, which were usually set over wide hearths and provided both heat and cooking space, were hardly efficient and much smoke still escaped into the rooms. A French scientist, Louis Savot, did experiments on chimneys in the sixteenth century and discovered that a narrow chimney was more efficient, and that the smaller the hearth the more heat could be reflected from it. His broad conclusion was that you could get more heat and less smoke from a smaller fire and narrower chimney. This must have seemed counterintuitive, and at the time his research was not widely recognised; his ideas had to hang fire for a century and a half before they were fully appreciated. One other reason for the lack of enthusiasm for this theory was because there was also a tradition of hanging a large pot over an open fire and fire users at the time were reluctant to give this up.

As we have seen, part of Franklin's ambition in building his Franklin stove in the 1740s was to eliminate the escape of smoke which became even more troublesome and toxic when coal started to replace wood as fuel. Around this time, Benjamin Thompson, known as Count Rumford, enters the stage with a determination to solve the chimney problem. Rumford was an American-born, British scientist whose major contribution to physics was a new and wider understanding of thermodynamics and insulation which equipped him well to study the workings of the chimney. Ever the inventor as well as the pure scientist, he can also claim to be the creator of the percolating coffee pot. In his fourth essay entitled 'Of Chimney Fire-Places' he writes:

> The plague of a smoking chimney is proverbial; but there are many other very great defects in open fireplaces, as they are now commonly constructed in this country, and indeed throughout Europe, which, being less obvious, are seldom attended to; and there are some of them very fatal in their consequences to health; and, I am persuaded, cost the lives of thousands every year in this island.
>
> Those cold and chilling draughts of air on one side of the body while the other side is scorched by a chimney fire, which every one who reads this must often have felt, cannot but be highly detrimental to health, and in weak and delicate

constitutions must often produce the most fatal effects. I have not a doubt in my own mind that thousands die in this country every year of consumptions occasioned solely by this cause, – by a cause which might be so easily removed! – by a cause whose removal would tend to promote comfort and convenience in so many ways!

His experiments involved building chimneys of different shapes and sizes, recognising that if a narrow point, or 'choke', was introduced, then the rising gases would speed up as they passed through it, creating an enhanced 'draw'. He described it as a device to 'remove those local hindrances which forcibly prevent the smoke from following its natural tendency to go up the chimney'. This helped the air and gases to rise quickly up the chimney, instead of leaking into the room. The angled sides of the reduced fireplace also acted as reflectors, throwing more heat into the room. He left readers of his papers that he was in no doubt how chimneys should be built:

I have abundant reason to think, that if, in constructing or altering chimney fireplaces, the rules laid down in my essay on that subject are *strictly* adhered to, chimneys so fitted up will very seldom be found either to smoke, or to throw out dust into the room; and should they be found to have either of these faults, there is a remedy for the evil, as effectual as it is simple and obvious: Bring down the mantle and the throat of the chimney lower; and if it should be found necessary, reduce the width of the opening of the fireplace in front, and diminish obliquity of the covings.

HOW CHIMNEYS WORK

There are two words that are quite distinct and yet often confused – flue and chimney. It is worth knowing the difference for if you are planning a new installation these two terms will crop up. However, even in official documents, the two may be confused.

The flue is the void through which the smoke and gases are released into the atmosphere. If you stand beneath your fireplace and look upwards, the space that you are seeing is properly called a 'flue'.

The structure around your flue most likely will be built of brick or stone. This is the chimney. So the chimney is properly described as the structure that surrounds one or more flues. If you have a house with several fireplaces emerging as a collection of chimney pots on the roof, strictly speaking you will have several flues but only one chimney.

YOU NEED SOME TOOLS

Don't worry, the tools you need are cheap and simple, but having them ready to hand will make burning wood less of a chore. Start with a poker, which is the simplest but most versatile of the wood-burner's equipment. Pokers made for coal fires tend to be straight, but one with a right-angle bend, or even a hook, can be useful when tending a wood fire, arranging logs or moving the ash around. You might decide that a pair of tongs would be useful for moving smaller pieces of wood around the firebox, and when building and lighting a fire when you might want to move around some of the hot ash left over from the night before. Inevitably, you are going to spill some ash on the hearth, for which a hearth brush and shovel will be required.

You will also need that small shovel when you eventually have to remove some ash, though don't do this too frequently. A modern stove will most likely have an ash pan but be aware when emptying it that even when a fire appears to be stone cold, within the pan can be ash hot enough to ignite paper – a problem if you are putting it in a waste bin, less of an issue if you are adding it to a garden compost heap. It can also be dug straight into the soil where it adds potassium, lime and other trace elements.

A small device, rather like a hoe, can be useful if you are trying to keep a fire smouldering through the night. For this you will need to cover with ash any holes that might appear in the grate, if your stove has one. This reduces the flow of air to the firebox and prevents rapid burning.

A good, strong leather glove or gauntlet should always be within reach. Stoves can get very hot and those with poorly designed handles can burn you if you try to open them with unprotected fingers.

All this might sound rather fussy but it is an important part of becoming a professional wood burner.

LIGHTING A WOODSTOVE

You are giving birth to something that will turn into a living thing, becoming your friend and companion as the night lengthens. The lighting of a stove should be approached with due respect.

Let's assume that the wood you intend to burn is properly dry, and that you have a bundle of kindling which is even dryer than that. If you are able, store your kindling indoors, somewhere warm. If you have room for a basket not far from your stove, so much the better. If you buy newspapers, you can use those to start the fire although be aware that something has changed about the way newsprint has been produced and many report it harder to ignite than it was twenty years ago. Glossy magazine paper is very difficult to set light to. Downloaded newspapers read on tablets are not much use either. Newsprint may soon become a thing of the past and then we will have to resort to the firelighter, of which there is an increasing choice.

The most commonly found is the ZIP firelighter, which is a small, solid block with its characteristic paraffin smell which can transmit to your hands, although they can come individually wrapped which overcomes this problem. Newcomers to the fire starting game are 'flamers', which consist of a straw rope soaked in candle wax. These are gaining popularity and have none of the odour problem.

If you have no paper or firelighter, you can carve yourself a 'fuzz stick'. Take a piece of straight grained kindling and with a sharp knife make downward cuts at an angle into the wood, being careful that the shavings remain part of the kindling. Make several of these. By increasing the surface area of the kindling, you will find that it can be lit quite easily with a match and several together will quickly take hold.

Before lighting the fire, the most important step is to make sure that all the stove's ventilation holes are fully open to allow the maximum draught.

THE BOTTOM-UP FIRE METHOD

This is the simplest way to light a fire and all you have to do is arrange a fire starting block on the base of the fire and then build kindling over and around it in the shape of a wigwam to encourage the flames to rise, as we did with the outdoor fires. Light the block with a match and your kindling will soon catch light. You might have to leave the door open a fraction to encourage it. Once the kindling has well and truly caught light you can gently start to place your logs on top and, with the door still ajar if necessary, your logs will start to catch. You have lit your fire. Don't forget to close the door or the temperature of the stove can rapidly increase.

Although the simplest method of lighting a fire, it has a drawback. As the kindling starts to burn, it will tend to fall away from its original structure, the logs will collapse onto it, and the flames might go out leaving you with a smouldering mass, which can be difficult to turn into a flaming fire.

THE TOP-DOWN FIRE METHOD

This seems counter-intuitive for we expect heat, smoke and flame to rise and therefore we assume that in order to create a fire the ignition source must be at the base of it. The top down method turns this idea entirely on its head.

You can use newspaper as a starter, if you wish, but as the paper is going to be on the top of the heap rather than at the bottom, it can tend to roll off. Instead, roll the sheets of newspaper then tie them into a knot and they will tend to stay in place. Again, ensure all the ventilation holes in the stove are open.

To build the fire, start with the logs but use ones which have been split, and are perhaps on the smaller side. Arrange these on the floor of the firebox. Then, place the kindling on top of these, and then some more kindling, finer cut, on the top of those so that going from top to bottom you go from the finest slivers of wood going down to the small logs at the bottom. Finally, on top of the kindling, place the newspaper knots and light them.

The advantage of this method is that there is very little smoke when the fire first starts, and the fire can't collapse on itself once the newspaper has burnt away, and you don't have to remember to put the logs on when the kindling has taken hold. There is not a stove owner who has lit a conventional fire and hasn't left the room only to remember to put the logs on long after the kindling has burnt away.

There is a third way which combines both these methods and which might be described as the 'sandwich method'. Lay two logs side by side with a gap between them into which you put the newspaper. Then lay the kindling on top, a bit like building a Jenga mountain, and a couple of small logs across the top of that. Building in a crisscross pattern ensures that as much of the wood's surface area is exposed to the heat of the kindling flame.

Wood-burners can come in all shapes and sizes.

There is much experimentation to be done until you arrive at a method that suits you and your fire, but somewhere within these three methods is one that will surely work for you.

HOW TO MAKE A FIRE LAST

If wood burning is your only source of heat then you will need to develop a technique which keeps the fire burning all night, ready to revive the following morning without relighting. This is not always easy and depends very much on the stove, and even the weather when a change in wind strength or direction can suddenly vary the rate at which a stove burns.

'THE TREE WHICH MOVES SOME TO TEARS
OF JOY IS IN THE EYES OF OTHERS ONLY
A GREEN THING THAT STANDS IN THE
WAY. SOME SEE NATURE ALL RIDICULE
AND DEFORMITY, AND SOME SCARCE SEE
NATURE AT ALL. BUT TO THE EYES OF
THE MAN OF IMAGINATION, NATURE IS
IMAGINATION ITSELF.'

WILLIAM BLAKE, 1799, 'THE LETTERS'

In principle, you need to get your wood burning, the stove refuelled, and then 'damped down' so the slow burn continues after the flames have disappeared. Try using something like a small hoe to bring the burnt pieces of wood towards the air inlets at the front of the stove, then pack the stove more tightly than usual with larger chunks of wood. These will burn more slowly and being closer together will not allow as much heat to pass between them – you don't want them to burn all at once. Now turn down the ventilation till the fire appears to almost go out. Go to bed.

In the morning, when you open the door, it may appear as though all your wood has been burnt to ash, but within that ash will be small nuggets of charcoal which will burst into flame given a decent draught of air. These tend to be found towards the back of the stove, furthest from the ventilation holes which always leak some air no matter how tightly closed. Coax these embers back into life, blowing gently on them perhaps, then add some kindling and start the fire all over again. When this resurrection works it is a rewarding experience, for the fire will blaze almost instantly, helped by the stove still being warm. You will feel you have brought an old friend back to life.

A SMOKING FIRE

A good fire should never smoulder. If it is producing only smoke and no flame it is no fire at all. All you are doing in pumping lukewarm contaminants into the atmosphere and getting little in return. Most stoves these days have glass windows so you can see exactly the state of your fire, but enclosed stoves can be harder to judge. It can be useful to fit a thermometer in the lower part of the chimney, which you can glance at now and again to see how well the fire is doing. Some attach magnetically to the flue without the need to drill holes. If it shows temperatures below 250°C then you are probably depositing tar in the upper reaches of your chimney. If your stove windows are smoked, or even covered in tar, then this is a good indication that at some stage your stove has been running too cool.

If your stove smokes when starting up, and assuming your kindling in bone dry, then you might simply have a plug of cold air sitting in the chimney, too heavy for the meagre amount of warmer air created at first lighting to shift. This is easily overcome. Simply place a sheet of newspaper over the top of the fire, not scrunched up but laid flat like a tablecloth. Let this catch light. It will produce a short-lived but decent amount of heat, which will push the blocked cold air skywards and then away you go. In some very cold countries, where temperatures are regularly many degrees below freezing, it is common for a wad of newspaper to be shoved inside the chimney and lit in situ. Without any warmth in it, a chimney will not work.

If your stove regularly smokes, it may be that there is not enough air entering the room. Modern houses are built to high insulation standards, which include reducing draughts to almost zero. Your stove might be a victim of a building fashion which we may live to regret.

The things to check if your stove smokes are:

Has the chimney been swept?
Is the stove to big for the size of the chimney or flue?
Is the chimney high enough to get a good draught, and if outside is it insulated?

Is enough air entering the room?

Is the top of the chimney fitted with a smoke arrester? This is usually a metal mesh intended to prevent any sparks from emerging for the chimney top, often found on thatched houses for obvious reasons. These can clog with tar, or birds might find them useful for nesting in the summer when the stove is not in use. I once had a stove in a small hut which would never draw. Once I discovered the spark arrester, which had turned into a solid block of tar, and removed it, the stove blazed fiercely ever after.

Chimney pots are complex and a law unto themselves, and to some extent things of great beauty. They appear to be the simplest of things but they are subtle in the ways they work, although few are able to describe their true workings. A good chimney sweep will advise you.

CLEANING STOVE WINDOWS

No matter how carefully you burn your stove, you are going to get some smoking of the glass and you are going to want to clean it. This is best done on a regular basis and not left for so long that you need to attack it with a scraper, which is not a good idea.

There are plenty of potions you can buy which boast of their cleaning power but sometimes the simplest is best.

Make sure the glass is cold – they can retain heat for a long time.

First of all see if much of it can't simply be removed with a damp cloth. If the window is only lightly smoked then this will often do the job. If that fails then everything you need is already at hand with no need to buy a thing. Take a piece of newspaper (from the pile you use when starting your fire) and dampen it, but don't get it wringing wet. Then, dip the newspaper in the cold ash in the bottom of the stove till you have a decent coating of ash on the wet paper. Then use it just like a sponge and go over the window in a circular motion gradually increasing the pressure as the smoke and soot comes away. Dampen the paper if necessary, and add a bit more ash. It is only mildly abrasive and will not mark the window. If you end up with a wet looking grey mess, this is good. Now take a clean and dry piece of newspaper and polish away the residue. Do it often, every day. If you are still getting heavy deposits on the window, your stove is not burning correctly or your wood is too wet.

KNOWING YOUR WOODSTOVE

If you don't develop a personal relationship with your stove, it's never going to be a happy marriage. You need to knows its ways, habits and idiosyncrasies so that you can tell, in every situation that might present itself, how your stove is going to behave. Will she burn steadily when the wind is in the north-east, or just sit there and smoke? If the wind goes round to the west will I be able to keep her going all night? And what about her diet? If I change from ash to beech will digestive problems flourish? Keeping and maintaining a wood stove can be made into a full-time hobby, and a rewarding one. If that is where your interest lies, then perhaps a modern, sophisticated wood stove is not for you – there might simply be too little for you to do. These stoves have been developed over the years to iron out as many of the difficulties as they can; they light at the touch of a match, never smoke, and give off more heat than the last generation of stoves could ever imagine. But they have taken away from the wood burning enthusiast some of the satisfaction of mastering their dampers and flues, doors and air inlets. So choose your stove carefully.

If you can get yourself to a position where you can hold an intimate conversation with your stove, where it tells you through its crackles and whooshes how it is burning, when you can read the cracks and creaks as it warms and cools, then you have achieved some of the deep satisfaction to be had from a wood stove. But it is a two-way relationship where the effort you make to understand and operate a stove is more than amply rewarded by that warm glow, which is like no other. Those of us who love our wood stoves find that our affection is well returned.

Hugh and Ced Wells – latest in a line of Charnwood stove makers.

THE STOVE MAKERS: HUGH AND CED WELLS

www.charnwood.co.uk

If ever you needed proof that the wood stove will always have its day, then hear the story of the Wells family, stove makers of the Isle of Wight. They are a family firm producing the Charnwood range, and can trace their business back nearly fifty years to an inventive grandfather who spotted an opportunity.

'He was an agricultural engineer,' explains Ced, 'not a stove builder. He lived close to the Charnwood Forest near Leicester where our stoves get their name from. In 1973, Dutch elm disease was ravaging the trees and there was lots of felled timber going cheap. This coincided with a spike in world oil prices and that's when he created a wood burner. He made it quite small, unlike the large Nordic ones, and he took it to a show and got orders for twenty of them. That's how it began.'

Hugh explains how when bad times hit, people revert towards certainties, and wood carries that promise of never letting you down.

'His early stoves were simple things. The glass smoked up, they weren't very efficient, and they were enamelled, which was one of his specialities. (The company still makes enamelled signs for the London Underground.) But when things are bad, as they were in the recession of the late 1980s, people come back to wood. They always do. We always do better when the economy is not so good. History tells us that when the economy dips, stove sales go up.' Perhaps economic pundits would be better watching the wood stove sales figures than all those supposed monetary indicators to which we give such credence.

'Of course, we had a foot in two camps,' explains Hugh. 'We were a Leicestershire-based business in what was then a coal mining part of the world. And miners were given free coal and we provided the ideal stoves in which to burn it. It means that we've learnt more from a solid fuel burning tradition that the wood burning practices of the Scandinavians.'

Charnwood stoves established a reputation over the years, but the perfect storm of the 2000s recession saw them move up the league table. People realised that gas and oil prices could go up at the snap of an international finger, but the price of wood was much more stable.

'Everything came together. There was the carbon agenda which everyone was talking about, and we could show that wood burning was carbon neutral – for all the carbon dioxide emitted by the burning of a tree, a similar amount was absorbed by a growing one. People were also looking to save money which was another factor. It added up to wood burning becoming fashionable as well as "green" and economic – a blissful state of affairs for a stove maker.

'Fashion is quite important to us,' says Hugh, 'but economics are more important. And we don't like mild winters!'

Stoves have advanced greatly since the early examples, some of which are on display at the factory, and clumsy things they are too

Hand-built
stoves at the
Charnwood
factory, Isle of
Wight.

– all with a built in certainty that you will burn your fingers when you refuel them. 'Our new stoves are 90 per cent cleaner than the old stoves, and the particulates show that a modern stove emits 80–90 per cent less than from an open fire. We don't only have secondary burning of the smoke to extract the maximum possible heat, we now have tertiary burning.'

Although seen by some as a fashion item, stoves are generally reckoned to have a more serious purpose, and that is reflected in sales. 'People don't always buy on looks. A stove has to do the job they're asking of it, and they want one that burns less fuel and produces more heat. They also want to buy from someone who can give them a lifetime's service with spare parts. A stove can be with you for a substantial part of your life.'

I ask what mistakes people made when buying stoves.

'You've got to get one the right size. Get one that's too big and you'll get through loads of wood and it will simply be too hot. If you have a smaller stove you'll always be running it hot and that's not good for the stove or the chimney.'

We all agree on one thing – that there remains something primitive about burning wood for heat that will never be eclipsed. You have to make an effort to load it with logs, and make an effort to keep it going, for the satisfaction you get in return. It is a natural instinct to want to warm yourself and, as both Hugh and Ced agree, 'there are some people who have never sat in front of a flame and they don't understand that a modern stove is so much easier than the old ones – my 4-year-old lights ours. We all want something that is not merely about existing, but about living.'

Which is exactly what a wood fire is.

10 | Smoking

YOU MIGHT THINK that woodsmoke is a toxic nuisance to be removed from the fire with all haste and efficiency; or, like many of us, you might never miss an opportunity to sniff the air if there is a wood fire nearby, despite the doom mongers. We taste the air as carefully as a vintner takes his palate to the claret decanter. Was it apple, or a bit of old beech? Certainly not pine, too feeble a scent for that. No, it was a hardwood, that's for sure. And so we go on, playing our games, mildly intoxicated, getting high on the smell of burning wood.

And then there's smoked food. There can be hardly a meat-eater alive who has not salivated over smoked ham or chicken. What about kippers, which are smoked herrings, or those tasty Arbroath smokies, which are modest-sized smoked haddock? And then there are bloaters, which are smoked herrings without the innards removed, giving them a gamey flavour. Even non-meat eaters might have enjoyed a smoked egg or smoked cheese.

As far as I am concerned, the smoking of food is another good excuse to light a fire. Even in the summer, when the domestic wood burner lies cold and idle, you can always find some morsel that will be enlivened by a bit of smoke, and that's the only excuse you need to start gathering kindling and wood with renewed excitement.

We have an old smokehouse in our village and it is often confused, from the outside, with a public lavatory. It sits by the harbour mouth, watching the tide go by. It has probably stood there for generations as the fortunes of small-scale fishing have ebbed away

The old village smokehouse by the sea.

First lighting for cold smoking – note the newspapers are in no danger of catching fire.

and left it largely forgotten. But some are still fond of it, and Luke offered to light up.

You do not need a smokehouse of this size or construction. You can make one from an old dustbin or an oil drum. But what you must decide – and it is hugely important – is whether you want to hot smoke or cold smoke your food.

If you opt for hot smoking it is easier, for then you are merely cooking your food in a smokey atmosphere. There's not much more to it than that. You can do it on one of those barbecues with a domed lid by getting it up to a decent cooking temperature and adding some damp hardwood sawdust to created a dome full of smoke. An average temperature for a hot smoker would be somewhere between 50 and 80°C. This is not a cookbook, but it goes without saying that cooking temperatures must be as strictly observed as

Cod and
herrings on
tenterhooks.

when cooking conventionally: there is nothing about smoke which will kill off any bugs in your food. That is why both fish and meat are usually brined before smoking.

Cold smoking is more difficult. The temperature must not exceed 30°C, and if less than that then so much the better. Smoking cold is where you are trying to impart smokiness to the food but you are not cooking it. Once smoked, it will still need to go through a cooking process, with the exception of some fishes, such as salmon, which can be eaten raw after smoking. The usual food safety advice applies.

Achieving cold smoke is not easy. It has to be allowed to rise from a fire that is only just burning and so is providing little heat. Travel is good for smoke since it will cool as it makes its way, which explains why our old smokehouse is so tall. By the time the smoke reaches the top it will be as cool as the air outside. There are a variety of cold smokers that you can buy, and all make the smoke travel some distance, usually through a tube, before it enters the smoking chamber. Cold smoking can be a slow process, taking up to a couple of days in some cases, or even longer if you allow the fire to go out and have to relight it. Keeping a fire at a steady smoulder, producing clouds of smoke but little heat, is an art in itself.

Forty-eight hours will give a deep, rich smoke.

Choosing the wood is, of course, a major decision. You should never smoke over pine for it is simply too full of tar and the resulting food will taste like it. Hardwoods are best, and the less dry the better – entirely contrary to usual fire making practice – because they will then burn slowly, hissing now and again but, most importantly, giving off plenty of smoke and not much heat. Alder is good for smoking, and fruit wood trees such as apple and plum can give a luxurious smoke. In the USA, Hickory is the wood of choice.

Luke lit our smokehouse with sticks and newspaper, waited till it was blazing, then added a few chunks of oak from Crispin's wood (see p 71). The flaming tinder soon ignited the wood – possibly a little too soon, as the oak was dry and we soon had a roaring fire. This is exactly what we did not want, so Luke smothered the flames with some hardwood sawdust and this did the trick. It soon became as thick as an old-fashioned London smog in there.

Some years ago, before he died, I went to see a professional smoker at work. Like us, he learnt it by trial and error, with a lot of error to begin with.

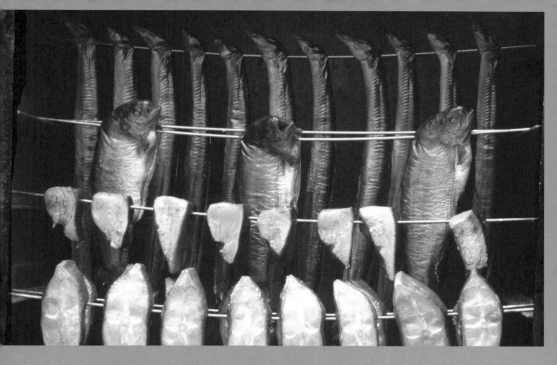

THE SMOKER: STEVE RICHARDSON

Richardson's Smokehouse, now sadly closed, was in Orford on the Suffolk coast, a few miles south of where our village's smokehouse stands. It sits amongst a land of marshes, wide vistas and open skies where the smell of the sea never leaves the air. In a narrow backstreet was where Steve Richardson chose to build his smokehouse. It was a cold January morning when I called. A brisk northerly wind fresh off the saltings cut through the town and blew the smoke from the smokehouse across the neighbouring houses as if it were trying to smoke them too. In the kitchen, mackerel were being washed in a huge sink, pheasants and duck were swilling around in brine tubs, and every time the kitchen door opened a blast of escaping oak smoke from the smokehouse next door filled the room.

'Shut the door,' cried Veronica, 'you'll smoke us out.'

'My grandfather, Frank Berrett, built the smokehouse,' Richardson told me, 'but I don't remember too much about it. Frank was a grand old boy. He was the local slaughterman and the baker. He was a fisherman too. I can remember sticking my head in the smokehouse once, when I was very young, and not being able to work out what the smell was. Of course, it was the oak. I know that now. I did a spell working on the oilrigs. Then I was out of work. There used to be a folk night on a Sunday at the local pub and I used to smoke a bit of mackerel and stand outside the pub selling it. That's how my smoking business started. It wasn't easy. I used the old smokehouse to start with, till the door fell off. I used to boil the hams in a Burco boiler! Can you imagine it? With a friend we designed a smoker but I never learnt anything off anybody, I learnt it all myself. When I started, I used to hang the kippers on the hot side and I couldn't work out why, when I went in the next morning, all I had left were heads hanging from the hooks. Too hot, you see.'

His smokehouse was the size of a pair of outside lavatories, built side by side with two doors, which were a tight, fit, but not smoke-tight. Thick lumps of tar, deposited by the escaping smoke, slithered slowly down the doors. Richardson, wearing a triangular wooly hat stained with tar and smoke, opened the door. A wall of oak smoke fell towards us and as it cleared, the simple burner could be seen in the shiny blackness of the smokehouse. It was no larger than half an oil drum with a vent at the bottom to control the draught, and a lid with holes which, by turning, would allow the wood to blaze, or smoulder to produce smoke.

'I always use oak. Green as hell. There's no thermometer, no temperature gauge. It's all done on the nose. A smell will just drift across and I'll think to myself, "Yes, that's done".'

On the hot side of the smokehouse sat a dozen chickens, a score of partridge. Through a letterbox in the wall seeped surplus smoke, cooling as it went, and here would hang hams – if he had the room for them – or sausages, prawns, kippers or even a Stilton cheese.

Back home, Luke and I had a few herrings, caught back in the summer, and a lump of cod bought from the local fishing fleet. It was part of the curing and smoking process that any fish had first to be cured in brine.

Richardson's
Smokehouse

The brine is a simple salt solution, but the strength of it is important. To get it right, drop a potato into the water as you add the salt. Keep stirring till it has dissolve and observe the potato. Once it starts to float your brine is strong enough. Leave your fish in it overnight, and rinse it before hanging it on the tenterhooks – from which comes the old expression.

We found the smoke fiendishly difficult to control. It was easy enough to create a blast of it, but maintaining a constant, steady flow was almost impossible unless we sat by it all day. So we took it in turns, returning every four hours till we guessed the fish to be smoked, largely by the colour on the outside. When it eventually hit the pan and was eaten with little more than bread and butter, it did not disappoint.

11 | The Modern Way to Burn Wood

YOU COULD SAY that the future of the wood fire has never been cosier. Half of Europe's renewable energy comes from wood-burning (*The Economist*) mostly as 'biomass', another name for wood. But leaving aside the increased interest in wood-burning as a sustainable source of energy, when it comes to the domestic scene wood is reverting towards its natural position as the fuel of first choice for anyone seeking the experience that the electric or oil driven heating system cannot offer. It would, of course, be fanciful to suggest hydrocarbon fuels were going to be consigned to the back burner anytime soon, but the numbers are impressive. According to the Stove Industry Alliance (SIA), a UK body representing stove makers and those with an interest in wood burning in the UK, 200,000 homes installed wood stoves in 2016, which showed a 20 per cent increase on the previous year. Apart from wanting to bask in the warm, yellow glow of their wood fires, these customers must be persuaded by the fact that a wood stove is 77 per cent cheaper to run than an electric stove for the same output, 29 per cent cheaper than gas, 43 per cent cheaper than oil and 50 per cent less than LPG (SIA figures).

All that good news occurs even before you get on to the reduced carbon emissions. So your pocket feels reduced pain and your conscience troubles you less; you have warmer days and sleep more soundly at night. Pleasant thoughts to have while the logs crackle. Scientific journals, meanwhile, branch out in all directions, some naming wood as 'fuel of the future' others debunking the thinking that says forestry can ever be carbon neutral. These massive questions need not trouble us as we sit before the smouldering embers, for we can at least be certain that by burning wood we are doing less damage than by employing any other method of keeping us warm. Let it rest there.

Bringing it back to our own hearth, and our own commitment to burning wood, the future will simply rest on whether we can get enough decent wood to burn. We have seen the efforts that the forester must make to grow it, the wood merchant to cut and split, and the work that we must do with axe in hand if we want to play a full part in the wood burning experience. But in the end, no matter how hard we work and how much sweat we expend, unless the fire delivers heat and glow then it is quickly going to go out of fashion.

In other words, we need good wood. Good wood makes great fires, and lousy wood makes no fire at all. If there's one lesson to be learnt from this book so far, that is it. And the principal quality that makes a lump of wood good or bad for burning is how much moisture it contains. Those old poems, which proclaim ash to be the king of fuels and alder to be the clown, are indeed true if the wood is freshly cut and still damp. Get the moisture out of any wood and it will burn nicely. Ash was only at the top of the tree, so to speak, because it carries less moisture than any other tree when first cut, so it is always going to burn best in the hands of an impatient fire-maker.

But now dry wood is within reach of all of us who no longer have to rely on the lad who plonks his load of logs on your drive and scarpers before you have time to quiz him about how long it has been stacked, and when was it split. It is called kiln-dried wood and those who have used it rarely use anything else, some calling it 'rocket fuel'. Traditionalists will shun it, claiming that air-dried wood properly cut and stacked will burn just as well – and this is true. But we live in impatient times and kiln-dried wood might be the thing that finally persuades the doubters that burning wood is the way forward in terms of economy, environment and effort.

THE WOOD DRIERS: GEORGE AND NIC SNELL

www.certainlywood.co.uk

If you want to find a rural innovator, then the best place to look might be in the direction of a farmer who is looking for new ways to make money on their land. This was the dilemma presented to George and Nic Snell, brothers who worked a Herefordshire family farm growing soft fruit and grass on which to graze cattle. Their father, Hugh, had been what George describes as 'a bit of an entrepreneur'.

'There was a man in the village making kindling. He used to make it out of old pallet wood. He had a pair of pliers to pull the nails out and sold the kindling to local garages. Dad saw this and thought there might be a better way of doing it. So he bought old boards, cut them and dried them, and made better kindling that way. That's when the idea of drying first appeared on the farm. Then father got interested in poplar tress, planted them all over the country thinking that he could eventually fell them and sell them to the match-making business and make his fortune. It was his passion. He planted 3,000 hectares of them. But by the time the poplars had grown, the match factory had closed and the round-the-world cruise he expected his poplar trees to fund never happened. So he had to find a new outlet for his poplars and that's how he got into the plywood business.'

This was important to the future of the farm in ways that could never have been predicted, because, although the plywood business never took off, the idea of putting wood through a drier to reduce its moisture content – which he'd first come across when making kindling – could later be developed. 'It's where it all started, really,' explain both Hugh and Nic, who are now running the largest kiln-dried wood business in the UK. 'He wanted a faster drying machine than the one he had, and he found an inventor in Worcester who claimed he had a working model of such a thing in his garage. It didn't look much more than a box, but all he had to do was upscale it.'

You need to understand that happens when wood dries, and the Snell brothers explain it like this: when you first place a piece of wood in a heated environment, the temperature of the wood rises

George and Nic
Snell – pioneer
kiln driers.

only very slowly as the moisture within it absorbs the heat, and eventually turns to steam. Once most of the moisture has gone, and when the moisture content has dropped to below 20 per cent, less energy is absorbed by the wood and the temperature of the oven will quickly rise without any more energy being applied. They learned this the hard way. 'I came down one Sunday morning and the whole drying oven was on fire. The wood had over-dried and gone into spontaneous combustion. It's pretty stressful, but as we've developed the technique we've had to get used to a fire now and again.'

The steep learning curve having been successfully climbed, they refined their technique to be able to dry a load of wood within forty-four hours when others were taking a week. 'We are the first in the UK to do that,' boasts Hugh, 'if not the world.'

The entire operation of their company, Certainly Wood, remains unseen from the road and you might never guess it was there. But the clue is in the air, which smells not of acrid woodsmoke, but is sweeter and more scented. This is the fine odour of drying, rather than burning, wood. Once you enter the old farmyard, you see buildings that once housed unprofitable cattle, now home to mountains of valuable wood. There are tree trunks stacked high, like the mightiest forest laid low by the ultimate storm.

'Beech is our first choice of wood,' says Hugh. I express surprise, remembering those old rhymes, which gave the number one slot to ash. 'No, not ash! Burn beech every time. We don't make the mistake of buying it by the ton, because that way you are paying good money for water. We buy it by volume, and that way we get good value because oak and beech will give you twice as much heat as other woods, because of their density. I can source 19,000 tons of wood a year, all within a 100-mile radius. I go to the big timbers auctions in Cirencester, but we are mostly buying from estates – buying standing trees which we select and then get estimates of their volume.'

I ask if there will soon be no trees left if he goes on like this? 'We only buy thinnings,' he insists, and goes on to explain the deficiencies of current forestry practice. 'You've got to plant 100 trees to get 10 good ones, trees that will produce timber for construction, or furniture. The rest of them you've got to take out

The wood yard at Certainly Wood – entire trees destined for kiln drying.

and these are the thinnings. That's what we buy. And do you know what? Two years after we've taken those trees out you would never know they'd gone, and the trees that are left can breathe and start to flourish.' This is clearly a win for all sides.

Both brothers are strong supporters of managed woodland but recognise that public policy is not on their side. 'Woodlands are protected. Woodlands will always be woodlands. You can't just fell trees, you've got to get a licence. It's a brilliant system. And we will only buy from woods where there is a scheme of guaranteed replanting. But the government isn't interested in commercial, planted woodland and only want to create amenity spaces. The consequence of this is that in the interests of providing a "woodland experience" for tax payers, they are ignoring the true demands of producing wood.'

Hugh adds, 'The result of the present system, where planting isn't properly subsidised, means that we are going to end up with jungles, not forests. We are planting the neglected woodlands of the future. If we don't get planting properly, we'll run out of wood in thirty years.'

There is something about the farm that speaks of invention, and inspiration. Nothing here is bought off the shelf: old containers are refurbished to make the ovens, ringed with pipes that flow with superheated oil. They started with one kiln, sorted out the teething problems – like opening the oven one morning and finding the wood well on it's way to charcoal – and with that sorted are now running seven kilns full time. The burner that gives the circulating oil it's heat comes from the plywood industry and is complex, automatic and sophisticated; the machine that splits the logs works on brute, hydraulic force. This is a marriage of simple invention, complex engineering, and belief that removing six tons of water from every eighteen tons of raw wood will deliver wood worth burning.

And then the doubts start to cross my mind. Where is the sense in burning oil in order to make wood burn better? Where's the reason in that? And, worse, how can we ever justify loading lorries and sending them, belching diesel smoke, the length and breadth of the country carrying white, plastic sacks of wood. Aren't we taking logs of wood and bashing the environment about the head with them? Perhaps not.

A well-burning stove causes the least possible emissions. This is the modern way to burn wood.

'As far as the lorries are concerned, we are only making use of existing capacity,' Nic explains. 'It's a very carefully worked out logistical process to get the wood delivered in the most fuel efficient way. There would be no fewer lorries on the road if we weren't dispatching logs all over the country.'

'As far as burning oil is concerned,' says George, 'we don't actually burn any. And I'm glad. We used to but it was too expensive. So now we burn all our waste, that's wood waste, and that's where the heat comes from that heats the oil that in turn heats the kilns. But that oil doesn't burn, it's just circulating.'

I looked into the firebox of one of the heaters through a glass spy hole and saw the flames of hell. And I saw the wood offcuts, and the sawdust, and the sweepings, all of which would have once presented a disposal problem and have become a fuel - they're burning the wood we can't use, so we can burn the kind of wood we want.

These two brothers are not only businessmen; they are lovers of fires, wood fires.

'I love everything to do with burning,' says Nic. 'I haven't got any radiators in my house. We've got a wood-fired Esse stove for heating. We've got a fire pit in the garden. We cook over wood. There's something about the way people will sit and watch a flame in a way they won't take notice of anything else. Getting a few logs in, there's no better feeling in the world.'

HOW TO BURN WOOD WELL

You will find plenty of environmentalists who will want to pour cold water all over your wood fire. They will argue that the smoke does untold damage to public health, that the technology is ancient and should be discarded because 'solar is so very cutting edge'. As for the cutting of trees for wood (sharp intake of breath) that ranks alongside an act of environmental murder. All these complaints harbour a grain of truth, but there are strong counter arguments.

Let's deal with the smoke. Woodsmoke can carry either the most agreeable, inspiring scent of earth, or it can be the most suffocating filth your lungs can breathe in. Those who create the latter, and there are many of them, are doing wood burning no favours. These are the people who allow their chimneys to billow forth with black clouds of pollutant, which settle on their neighbours washing and creep in through the slightest crack in door or window. It is easy to make yourself highly unpopular by burning wood badly, and rightly so. The worst offenders are those who have been dubbed the 'recreational burner'. These are the ones who see the wood fire as decoration, part of the image and not the fabric of their homes. They probably don't even turn their heating down when the wood fire is lit. They take a superficial view – as long as it's cheering them up, that's all that matters. They will not have given thought to their stoves or chimneys, will not be using modern methods of efficient burning, and most likely will be burning their wood in an old grate designed for coal. A filthy, smoky fire will emit 20g to 60g of particulates every hour – a huge amount. But good wood, burnt in a modern stove, at a high temperature, will get that figure down to 7.5 (woodheat.org).

Nor will the casual burner have chosen their wood or their supplier well, and it is highly unlikely they will have gone to all the effort described in this book to get the very best out of a piece of timber that has been so long in the growing. That piece of wood has overcome so many natural obstacles before flourishing as a tree; the woodman has curated and cared for it till it is ready for the axe, and it is an insult not to burn it properly.

So the first rule of burning wood well is to think of it not as piece of decoration, but as important a part of your wellbeing as your running water or the fridge. You wouldn't suffer inefficiencies in either of those, and you shouldn't in your wood burning.

And we must accept that wood-burning can never replace conventional heating in towns, cities or high-rise apartments. It just can't. But that doesn't mean it has no place at all. Modern wood-burning stoves, built to high environmental standards, can reduce emissions to within the required city limits. Modern wood-burning is now employing some of the most advanced heating technology, and is not harking back to an inefficient past.

But what about the smoke? A report from the US Environmental Protection Agency said:

When the contributions of all the components of energy production for residential space heating and the atmospheric fate of pollutants are taken into consideration, wood combustion has the lowest greenhouse gas and acid precipitation impacts per unit of heat delivered among the energy options. Its fine particulate impact based on existing wood-burning appliances was the highest among the options.

Not good news regarding particulates, then, at first glance. But the level of pollution, as we have seen, can vary enormously with the way in which the wood is burnt. Black smoke consists of unburnt hydrocarbons, and the thicker and blacker the smoke the more stuffed with these hydrocarbons it will be. But if the fire is burning hot enough, these hydrocarbons, which are tar-like, rise from the wood and are burnt in that area of intense heat just above the flames. This is where they oxidise and break down into carbon gases and some water vapour all of which are hardly seen when they emerge from the chimney. It is a simple truth that a smoking fire is no fire at all. But a properly burning fire will emit the least number of particulates, and this is what modern stove makers try to achieve, but only if stove owners are part of the team too.

These are arguments which can go to and fro and views on either side can be extreme. But I have seen no figures which compare the effects of woodsmoke on health, compared with the damage done by particles emitted by vehicles. The equations which we currently believe to rule the behaviour of the environment now contain so many variables, that it is almost impossible to be certain of the 'right thing to do'.

I'll tell you my conclusion: Grow your wood responsibly, and replant what you remove. Cut it and dry it till it is almost begging to be burnt. Get yourself the most modern, efficient burner that you can and make sure the chimney is properly functioning.

Light your fire, sit back, enjoy the flames, and let that powerful medicine called peace of mind work its magic.

That's the modern way to burn wood. ■

Index

PLAYING WITH FIRE